1 front cover
1 back cover
sources p64.

62 pages of personal writings and sketches
23 notes

art
dreams   psyche
memorie   experiences
reflection   life

the written English alongside
it is not an exact translation
but its content is generated from the notes,
so, is a kind of convesation developed
in two languages by the same person.

created for MFA, Art, Society, and Publics [R&W/PP3] purposes
by Kristian Zara [Student (2016/17). University of Dundee, DJCAD]
start: 25.03.2017
end: 08.05.2017

I have searched myself.
Εδιζησάμην εμεωυτόν

These two words speak volumes. Self-examination is the hard-
est thing to do, something Freud had to learn slowly and he
spent much of his life doing just that. It is not a simple
truism that the unsearched life is not life at all.

It pertains to all men to know themselves and to be temperate.
Ανθρώποισι πάσι μέτεστι γινώσκειν εώυτους σωρονείν

To be temperate is the greatest virtue.
Wisdom consists in speaking and acting
the truth, giving heed to the nature of
things.
Σωφρονείν αρετη μεγίστη, και σοφίη αληθέα
λέγειν και ποείν κατά φύσιν επαίοντας

The words of Heraclitus, when he talks about eyes being better witnesses than the ears, bridge me with Paul Klee's depicting of the eye as a thinker (the thinking eyes), as observer. Thus, similarly, my eyes are continuously seeing, always searching since I opened them for the first time. Even when I'm asleep they are working and collaborating with what goes on in the universe.

The universe consists of two components; one is that of visible matter (nature) which is closer to my view and body, and the other is that of invisible matter (obscure nature) which stretches beyond the profound sky, and bellow the soil. By these two components is how I perceive consciousness (the known) and unconsciousness (the unknown), similar to the mind-desert consistency.

I'm part of the nature, consequently I'm one of its representations, consequently it would be wrong to think myself as a detached particle from it, especially when I see that inner self functions same as the universe.

To lead the imagination further, I think about the sun [the great sustaining force of life] and the moon too [that regulates the tides and establishes biological rhythm]; both stand in the depth of the space beyond the sky counting the rhythm of time. Their functioning explains exactly how images have the same effect in my psyche which operates mystically and continuously within the mind.

The reason why I'm attracted significantly by the images is the relation they have with the life experiences gathered so far. They are like soil from which most of my works originally grow.

Through these personal notes, I bring my writings as raw material (written in Albanian language) with an interpretation in English language alongside. By this I want to shown the hidden part of a reflective approach of an artist's psyche, and to make the reader think from a different angle, that is to say, a different observation of the same topic.

Also, throughout this book I want to show the very early material that appears before the development of each artwork, and how I deal, as an artist, with the complexity of the unconscious by focusing on the symbolism of images [influenced by C.G Jung's theory of symbols]. This outcome can be called too, as conceptual space of a conscious perception of the Cosmos related to images of the world within and without. In its content you will see directions rather than definitions.

There are some images that appear from the inner depth of the self, and repeatedly, they appear even when I'm awake. These images enclose many layers that I must unfold starting from the experiences of the past, forgotten memories to forbidden desires where they are linked to.

They are preserved in this obscure depth in the state of invisible phantoms, as they remain until I seek of understanding of their content by the necessity to express myself that has become a method to learning about myself simultaneously, for I'm driven by a conscious will to advance deeper into the unknown, [the consciousness is always employed and affected by the state of mind in seeing the many aspects of one thing, accordingly.

The consciousness like the retina of the eye, is engaged in filtering the experiences and everything that follows by bringing light into the unconscious.

All these seem like the waters of a swollen river.

imazhet që shfaqen në brendësinë e unit, dhe që
periodikisht riprodhohen edhe gjatë kohës kur syri është
zgjuar shumbëllityra të cilat të tregojnë dhe
të lidhin ~~edhe~~ me pjesët e shumta që përbëjnë
çdo përjetim. ~~the~~ ~~...~~ Të kuptuarit të këtyre
shumbëllityrave është rruga e cila vetëdija ~~...~~
merr sipas nevojave që uni ka.
~~...~~ Pshumbaj ti qëndron, zgjuar, i lidhur dhe i
zhytur në mendime, duke ngulur shikim tënd
tek gjithçka që shpaloset përpara teje, nga lart
poshtë dhe nga e majta në të djathtë. Rastësisht fkta-
për mendimin tim nuk ka iastëri sepse nëse ti
nuk adoronerr një vështrim kërkues, i cili fillon
dhe ka të bëjë me gjendjen mendore dhe shpirtërore
të ~~...~~ certit, nuk do vëri re gjërat të cilat
ndodhen përpara ~~...~~ teje ~~...~~ të njëjtën
mënyrë) të bie në sy një dritare- e cila
është e një dhome pa dritë ndezur duke kthyer etë
(obikanen në një lar pasqyre - ky shëmbëllehet
një shkallë që ~~...~~ diku në një plan tjetër
e në një venëndije krejt ~~...~~ nga ~~...~~ venëndija
jote apo e vetë dritares. Kjo shkallë është
e fshehur nga shikimi jotë, për kundvështrimi
jot me ndlihnda e ~~...~~ kënd pasqyrimit ~~...~~ dritares
bëjnë të mumbur reflektimin dhe zbulimin e
shkallës së "fshehur", gjithashtu ~~...~~ mënëlja
kortnese bashkë ne gjëndjen shpirtërore

-How does this process develop itself within me?

-What does it imply by its content?

SELF-REFLECTION

Naturalist Henry David Thoreau said: Man cannot afford to be a naturalist,
to look at nature directly, but only through the side of his eye.
He must look through and beyond her.

For instance, I'm awake, and immersed within my own thoughts, staring at everything in front of your eyes, from up to the down-side, left to the right-side, where everything spreads out its physicality…
  In a fraction of minute, I see a window -of a dark room- where I notice a pair of stairs reflected at. Normally, the stairs are hidden from my view, I cannot see them from this position, but by the glossy window they appear exactly before my eyes. Not much clearly shown by the window glass, nor that easy to be noticed by a distracted eye, but there they are by a reflection that becomes less or more obvious as the sun changes its mind continuously.
  Then after, at this point it becomes known to me. So, the same process seems to happen in my mind when an image appears.

But, Is this a state of self-awareness or just a normal continual mind-process that I haven't noticed before as I do now?

Whatsoever, I believe that one must turn the eyes inward to the self to become aware of this continual process in his daily life. This approach towards the inner has its own defence that one should deal with at first, then the greater self can be discovered; think about a big oak tree, its great shape, the years and its greatest force which operates under the soil.

There is also another component that springs out of the images, that of social-strata, and it seeks about attention. It can mirror something that is forgotten, but not lost; of something that once is understood it turns to valuable
element for the psyche, and the human being oneself, regarding to the outward behaviour, as well.

It is through art that I can explore further my inner, and to have an unconscious desire to experience
[or re-experience] the two worlds (within and without) which is more valuable than my achievements; much knowledge is gathered throughout the way of living.

Thus, is my creativity; alive, changing, growing within contradictions, bound by desires, and directed by an inner will to ''power''; it starts as a chaotic flow, then it becomes an analysis of the self and of the out world. Whether nature draws the birth of forms from the chaos -says Artaud- and so I draw the birth of my works from the chaos of images.

Each image is linked to itself and to the Universe
at the same time.
These two happenings
are very similar in their souls.

Eh, kur m'lidhen gjith turbllinat
n'kapakun e koks
e menja fillon e lun si era nepër
sokak
tuj vorbullit
tuj u përplas mur n'mur
sikur me shkly n'vete asht,
vendos
n'vatrën
e sqift tvet.

Sot, sis nach jacht
po asht' nach nd shpirt tem.
Asht e ashpën rruga
n'thellësi me zbrit
n'kjellësi meu ngrit.

29 12 16

O, when the clouds

    of the mass

       land as a hat on my wandering thoughts

                    And the mind
like the winds vagabondizes
around the alley borders

A spiral space over

    A slam from wall to wall

left

      as if it wants ripping out itself

                    placed
already...

Today, as happens outside,
so happens inside me

The path is harshly passable

In depth to descend

Into the hearth

In serenity to ascend

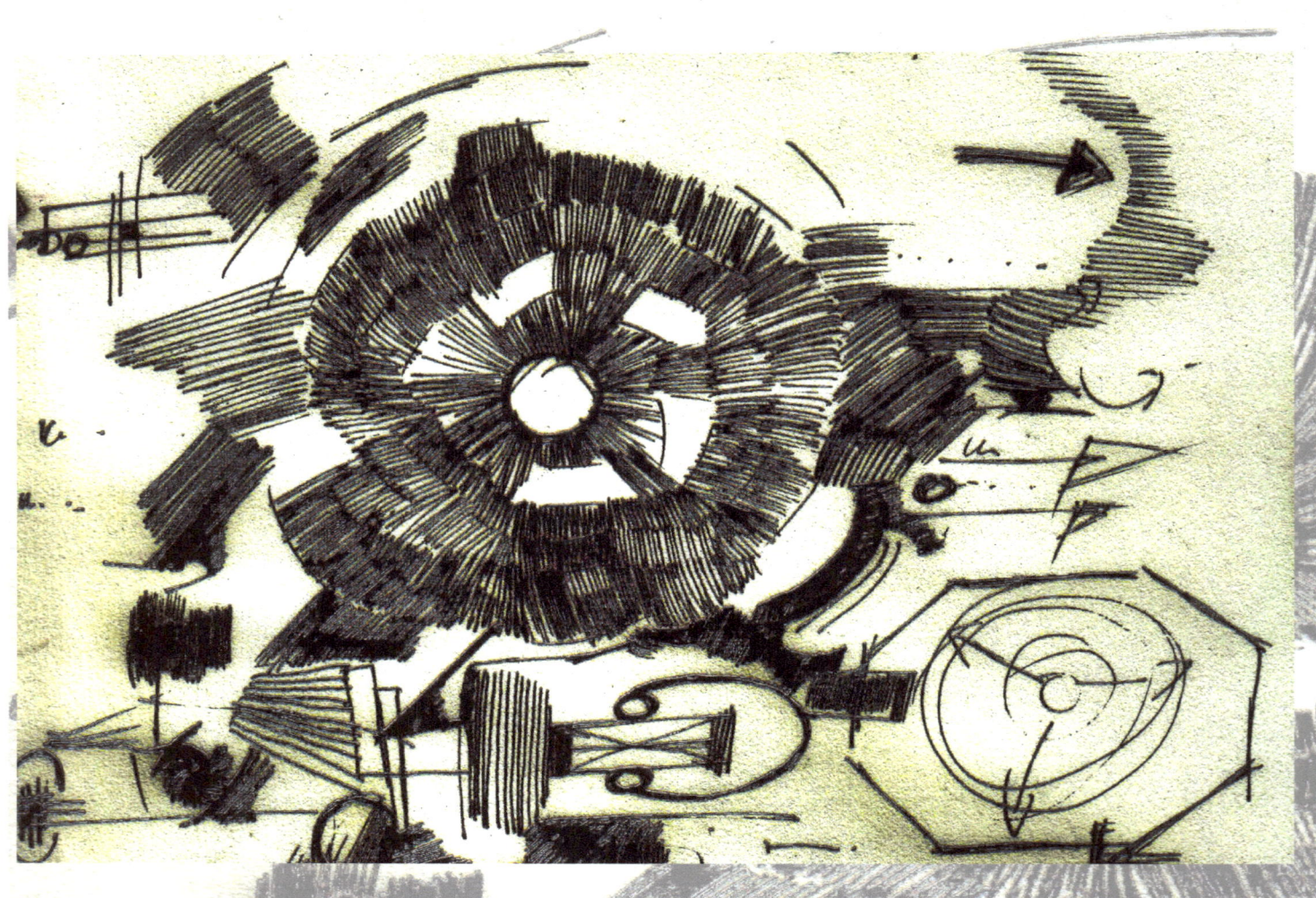

There has a travel throughout many degrees on the way thoughts
follow, therefore it would be the courage of the light that brings
its warmth into the cold night of inner winter.

From the 'sun of symbols' to the core of my 'inner power'.

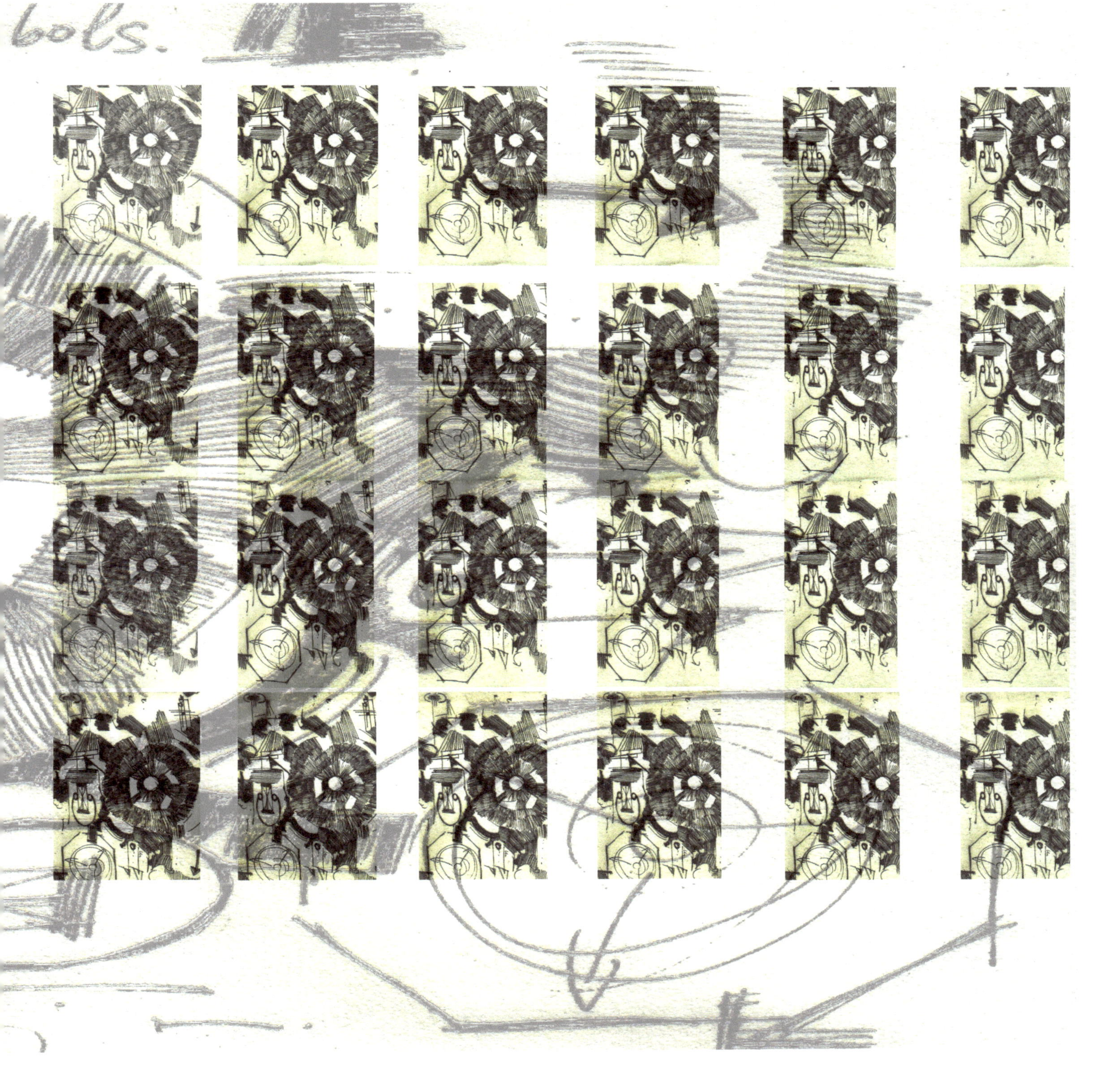
bols.

<u>Fire and Respect</u> [Gaston Bachelard] – The psychoanalysis of Fire.

The Prometheus Complex.

"Fire is thus a priviledge phenomenon which explain anything. If all that changes slowly may be explained by life, all that changes quickly is explained by fire. Fire is the ultra-living element. It is intimate and it is universal.

p.7.

Dielli i largët.

.2.

Atëherë Dielli është zjarr
zjarri është Diell
që të dyja janë burime
të dritës që na ndulon,
dhe na drejton
përgjat rrugës sonë.

Dheu bëhet më pjellor kur
pyelli digjet, krijon mundësitë
e një rifillimi të ri jete.

Zjarri është një nga elementet i prodhuar nga drita. Drita është rrezatimi i zjarrit të largët që ne quajmë Diell. Nëse bëjmë një eksperiment duke marrur një lupë dhe e vendosim përpara një letre, midis Diellit dhe letrës, do të shikojmë se lupa forcon dritën e Diellit duke e kaluar atë në anën tjetër, mbi letër, me një shumë forcë e cila do të bëj të mundur djegjen e letrës.
Lupa është ai objekt i cili bën të mundur dritën djegëse sikur burimi, i sa të është afër objektit që digjet, (letra).

.3.

– mundet kjo ndodhi të jetë metaforë
për atë që ka të bëjë me krijimin në art?
Të zbulosh çka në brëndësinë tënde fshihet
është njëlloj sikur ti vësh flakë të gjithave,
dhe ndase një dhe i ri krijohet për të mbjellur
ose mundësitë për vazhdimin e jetës bëhen edhe
më të shumta.
Pra një rrymë e re drite është ajo e cila i vë
flakën gjithë pyellit i cili është rritur gjithë
ato vite përjetimi, duke sjelur filiza të reja dhe
të freskëta. Kjo është në dëshirën time, nëse dua
ta shuaj apo të lë të digjet zjarri në brëndësinë time.

15 03 17

Fire is an element of light, and light is a ray from the fire… the furthest fire, so called sun. Whether we make an experiment with a paper and a loop which is placed between the sun and the paper, after a while the paper will get burned. The loop is like an enforcement for the sun ray, as if sun was closer to the paper. Thus, is one of the means of self-discovering, by the way the desire (loop) is placed between the unconscious (sun) and the conscious (paper) can be possible to strength the inner eye (knowing yourself). On the other hand, the stronger the inner eye gets, the more pain (burning of the paper) is seen. Nevertheless, a new soil will be discovered when you cross on the other side, and much joy is found there to spread the seeds of a deliberated self, the greater you become facing the inner world.

Sometimes, to discover what is hidden inside of yourself is like giving fire to all what seems to be there, perhaps new pos-sibilities will be uncovered though!

Thus, is how the knowledge comes as the light that kindle the fire which burns most of the old 'planted trees' of an earlier life of a man. Therefore, a different wind can only shake the mind-social-psychological-behaving barriers in order to change them.

[the soil becomes more fertile when it's burned]

[Can this be the same as the process of making oneself?]

The empirical knowledge brings a new platform of potential means for the future time. That is what I'm mostly searching for, a ''New Format''.

I would point out that self-exploring has a similar

aspect as the spontaneous way of working an

artwork that often happen to me. I mean, this force can spring out unexpected part of myself, and of which I'm driven continuously.

An uncontrolled force that engage the desire to gather more knowledge, which after becomes

a tool that cleans up little by little the unintelligible happenings. In many of my paintings, I've experienced the burning process within myself, where the unknow becomes intelligible and the old believes must change then, and

by letting it happen

(deliberation, spontaneous way of working) I have advanced, evolved my consciousnes, suddenly. For it is hard to observe,

and less tangible

to be run.

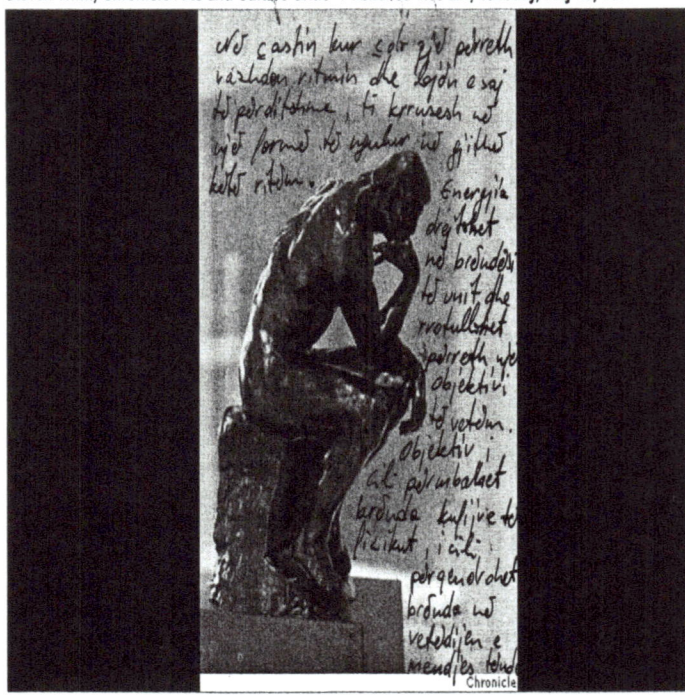

IMAGE 1 OF 2

photo illustration for Steven Winn column on unconscious thinking in art. Chronicle__COLLECTING12F-C-31JAN00-PK-JLT Rodin's 1904 sculpture "Le Penseur" is part of the collection of Allan Rappaport, M.D. of
... more

Part 2 of 2

"Time slows down," said Janet Bishop, curator of painting and sculpture at the San

Francisco Museum of Modern Art. "I'm enveloped. The painting I'm looking at isn't the

painting anymore. It becomes this place that's entirely other from itself."

Bishop was describing what happens to her in the presence of a 1969 Mark Rothko

canvas in the SFMOMA collection. "I could describe its color and its shape and its size,'

28 02 2017

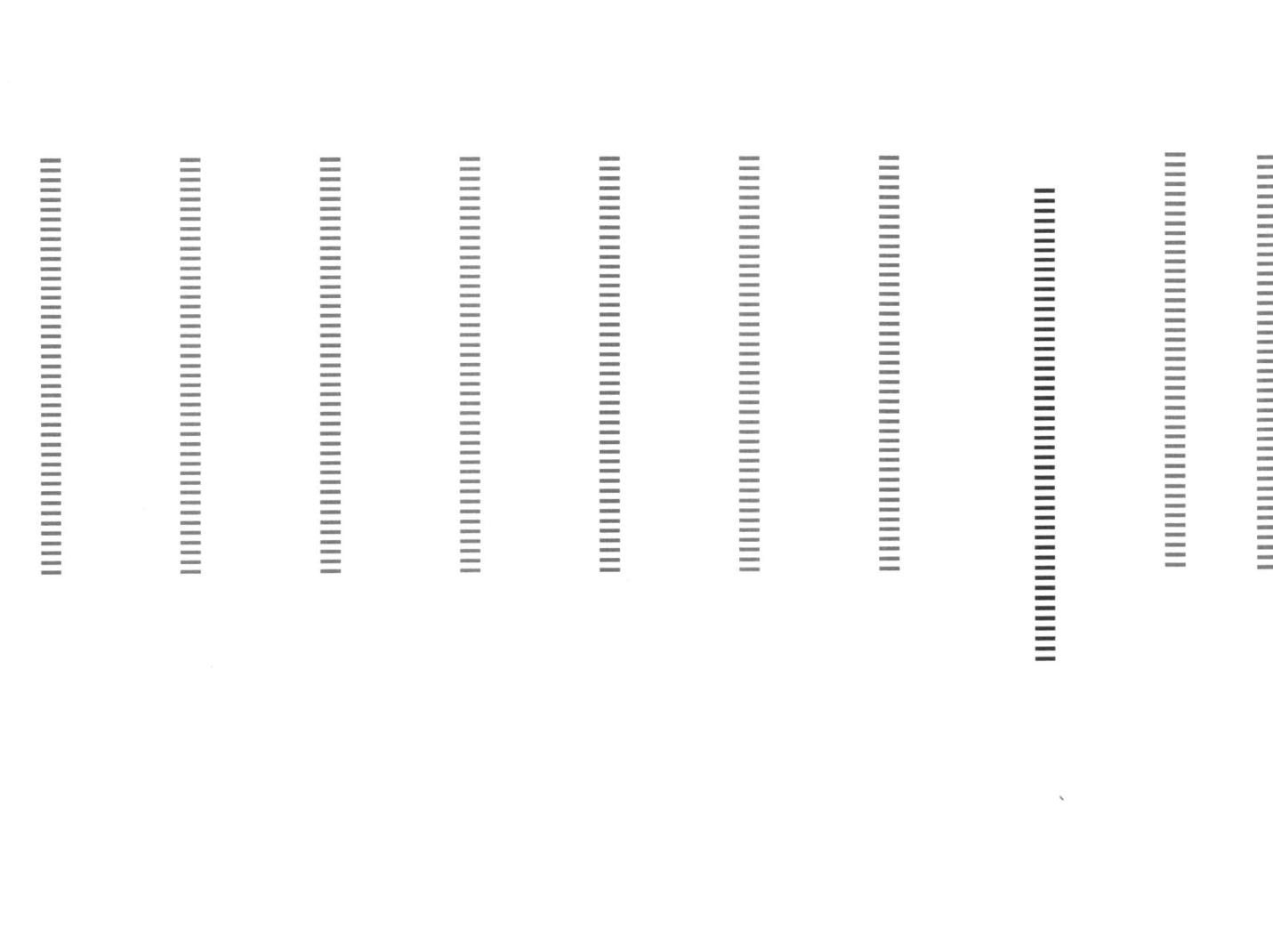

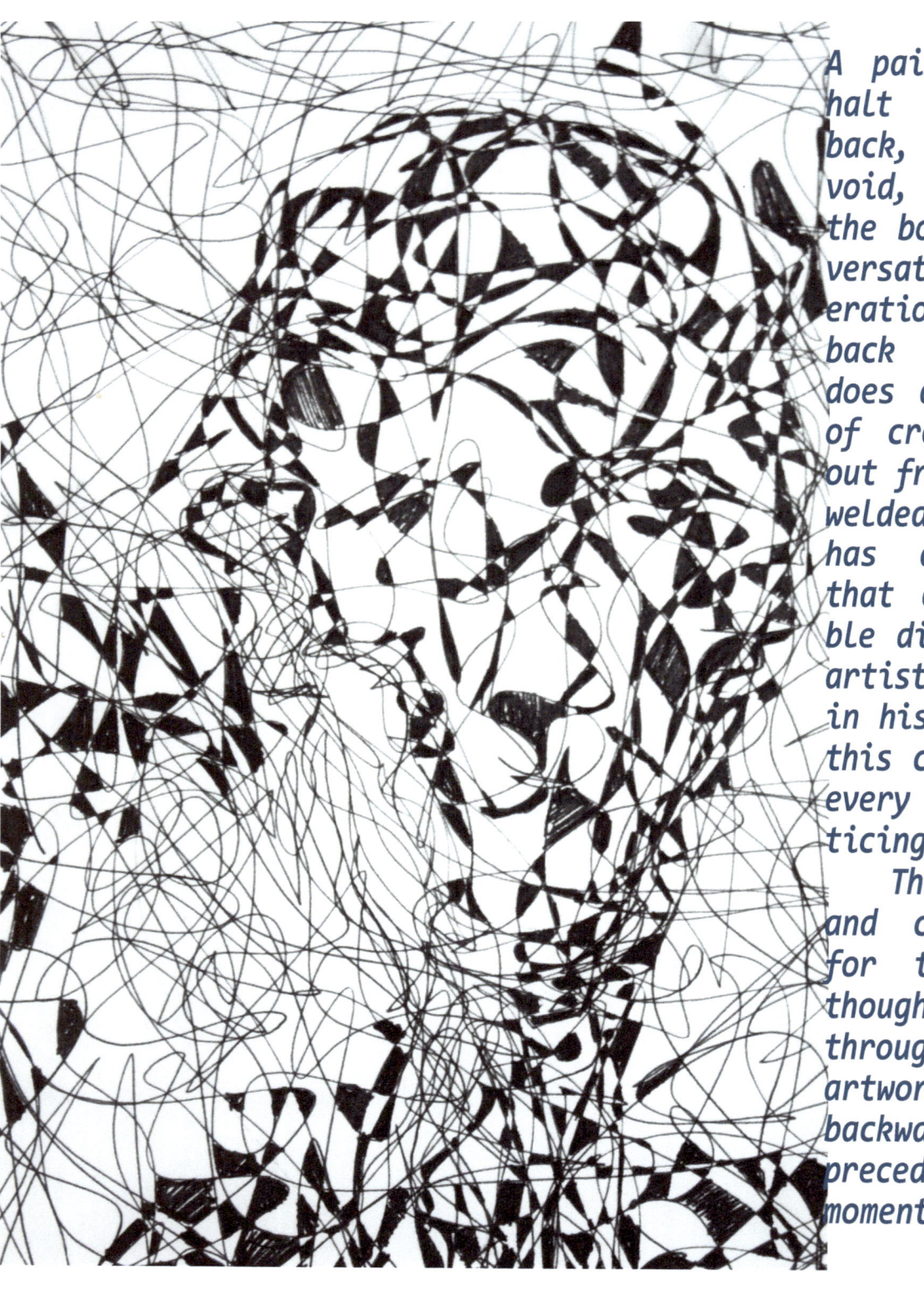

A painting itself is a halt in time, a going back, a jump into the void, is a flight outside the body, a oneself conversation, a war, a liberation, and a turning back again the artist does during the journey of creativity. It comes out from past and future welded together. There has a spinning force that creates an invisible dimension, while the artist is deeply involved in his ongoing journey, this composition happens every second without noticing about.

Thinking is creating and creating is means for the conversational thought oneself. The time throughout the making an artwork is like running backward, whereas, it precedes a very future momentum, literally.

Every added detail becomes past, whereas the end of a work remains as halt at a very moment the artist completes his purpose. I would say, a work is like a bridge that is a steadily concrete connection from A to B, and what's needed is the man who should just walk over it, freely.

Furthermore, a halt within our thoughts is, on the other hand, a recollection of memories, consequently this approach gives birth of new ideas. Is akin of signal given to the mind-core when we start working about an idea, and throughout the development of this idea many other layers appear by, and if we detach them from the main body then each of them become another idea itself.

Therefore it must be the need or tendency of the soul for developing further of human being, as well as very significant element in the artist's wold.

When I recall my personal memories,
then a mass of waves would fall towards
the present moment… the present that,
literally, is a consistency of past and
future times attached to the same body.
This mass of waves is the product
of a totality of an active current that
springs out from any experience
(consciously or unconsciously lived)
and its force has shown its effectivity
in my psyche regarding the degree of personal perception of the world. I've seen
this in my sensitivity about [Death], which
is one of the very strong experiences
of my childhood.

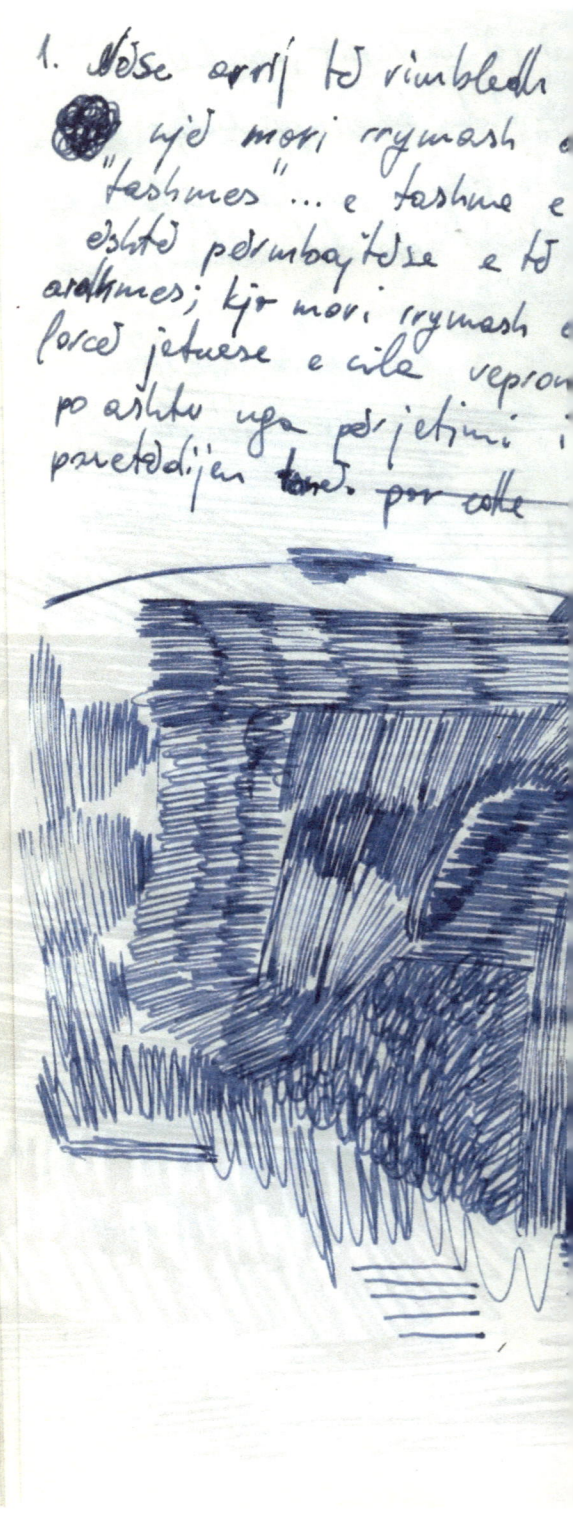

...alvardn, atelheve.
...vrdigine drej se
...f ne te vertete
...jese kaluar dhe e se
...yjd gjithesine e saj
...r mjet dhe vijedh
...la shenjet e tij ne
...e

Mbaj mend, kthjellshëm, se trupi dhe duart
ishin kaq të lidhura me melodinë sa
çdo gjë krijohej kaq lirshëm dhe spontan.
Madje, ndjenja e zhveshjes të trupit nga
çdo robe, ishte kaq e fortë, sikur kërkonte
të çlirohej nga kufijtë dhe vetë lëkura të
ndjente rrymën e muzikës drejtpërdrejt mbi
të. Kjo ndodhi, dhe vetvetja u gjend e zhveshur
lakuriq, duke kërcyer dhe duke krijuar
bashkë. me piktura një atmosferë, një
vapër të vetme në të përgjithshmen e saj.
Sot mund të them me fjalë të plota dhe
vetëdijshëm se ai moment ishte një kriji-
mtari e vetëdrejtuar "automatic working".
Una isha i drejtuar nga pavetëdija ime.

28.02.17

Another memory is that of a night when I was tying to paint the rhythm of music without any plan in my head, nor in my hands.

I remember well, that moment when my body and hands were
so much connected with the melody that I was listening to,
as much as everything was creatively free and spontaneous,
simultaneously. Even the feeling of nudity, movements,
and getting rid of any clothes was like becoming free of
any psychological obstacle. I felt so lost and far away
from the world, as if I've had desired it for long time.

-The sound of music is like the magician, who, by a little pendulum can cre-
ate seductive waves, which can transport you into other waters, and so others
will run after.

Or, I've been 'drunk' by the freedom of moment, and this can
be compared how mind works sometimes that makes you feel
and live the same thing differently again!

[we perceive by many sense perceptions or organs, which in combination with our experiences form a certain pattern in the psyche, in our soul; and the more we set our self to limitless possibilities, the more these patterns change. In art, it is seen throughout the development of a subject [Idea], technically, so called maturity of the artwork]

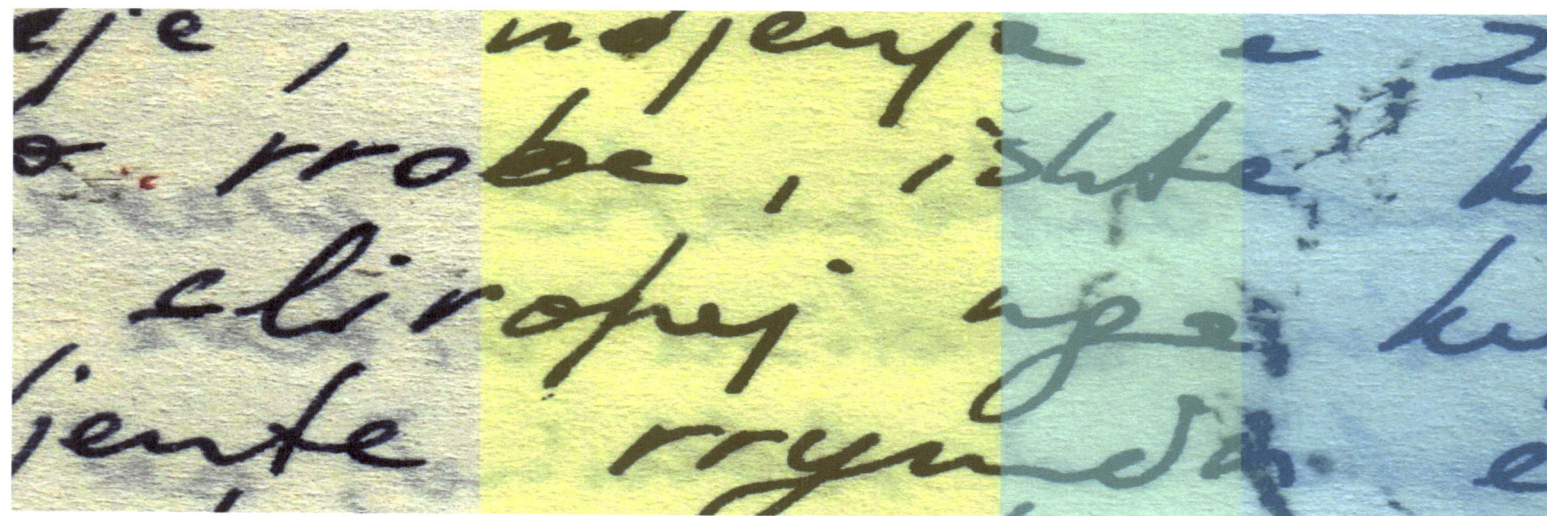

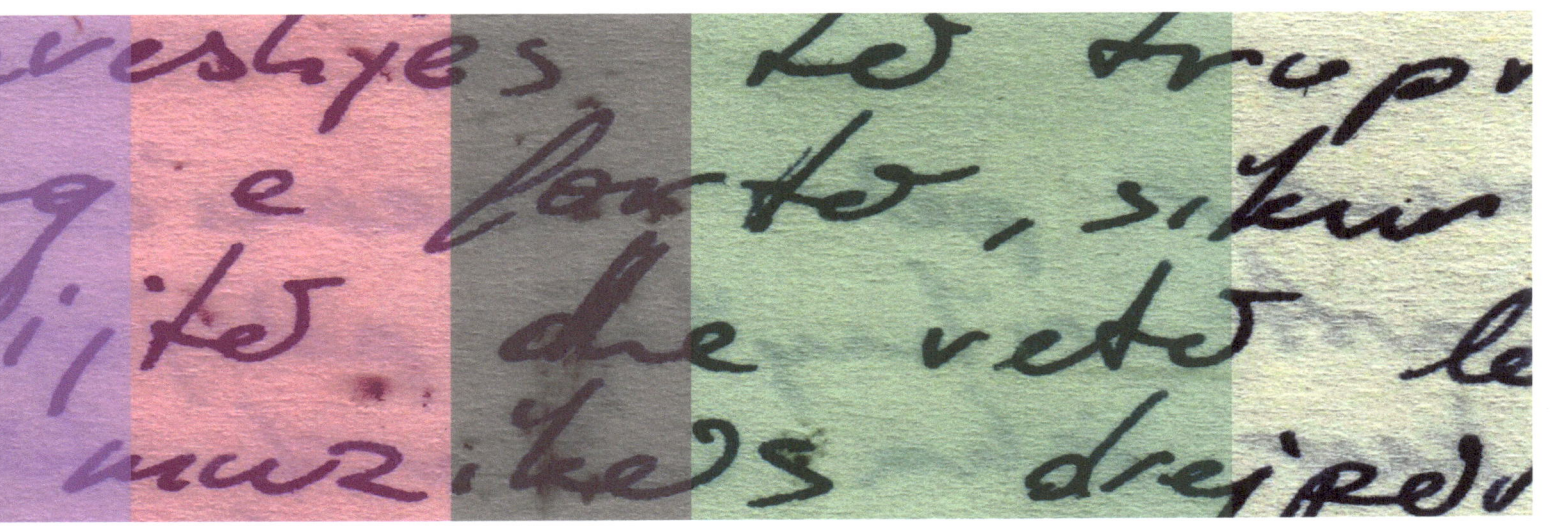

-I caught myself dancing alone and painting, whereas everything had happened unconsciously and I haven't noticed the works I've had done in one single night. Why and how the self does so? This desire [during the working time] to go away from the course of the conscience, and let things happen, makes me to turn the view to some of my dreams, in terms of exploring another aspect of the self.-

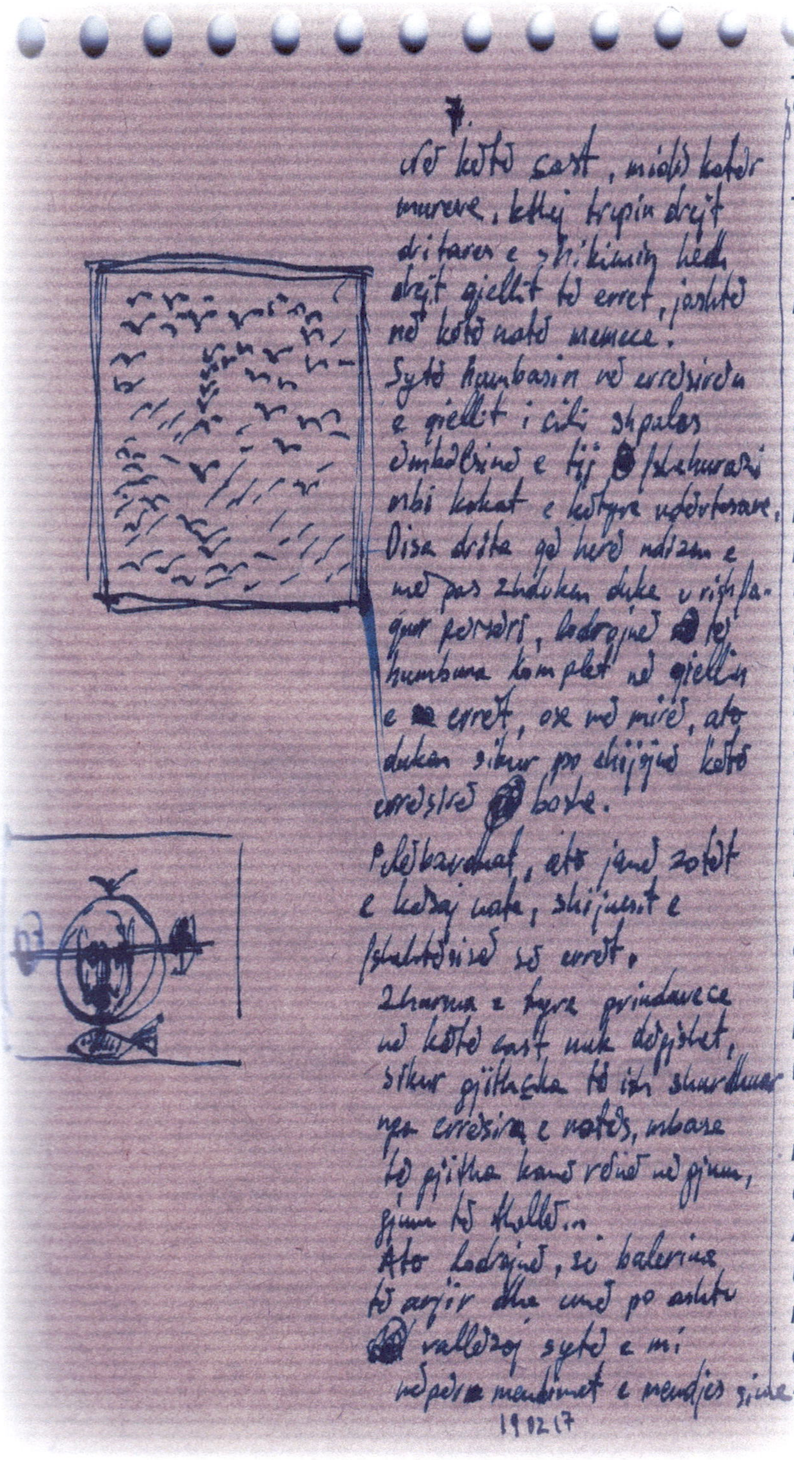

Thus, my sleep consists of fragile defence, it needs just a drop of light or a bit of sound to interrupt its course. I look at the sky, and it is dark, and profound. My eyes are lost, focusing on nothing; there is a beautiful black colour that lies silently above the buildings all over Dundee. It is so dark just like the 'black ivory' oil colour, and it feels like the time has stopped its course now and forever. There are some lights too, I notice, that appear and disappear and then reappearing again they form a web of twinkles, performing rhythmically a numinous dance in honour of the 'supreme leader' [the darkness]. Seagulls! They are seagulls, little gods of the sky, in this night and every night across, the savour of the obscure silence magically attired by the lights of the city bellow. The quarrelsome sound it has begun mute, as well as my breath, or I become deaf, for instance!

The citizens seem fallen into a deep sleep, a sleep without traces and faces, even their waves are retired tonight.

While, Seagulls are still dancing, as if were taught by the invisible Master to attract my view through their soothing movements, I feel like fallen slowly into my dreams again.

At the end I cannot resist, give myself up, and leave my thoughts flowing around my mind [I'm drunk by this lullaby tonight], among these walls of a temporary temple 'of the Psyche'.

''THere is
a gate
An uncontrolled gate
that opens
the way
to the
outer world,
by which
the inner
releases
its stories
Unconsciously
Spontaneously''

'Seagulls' everywhere around... .

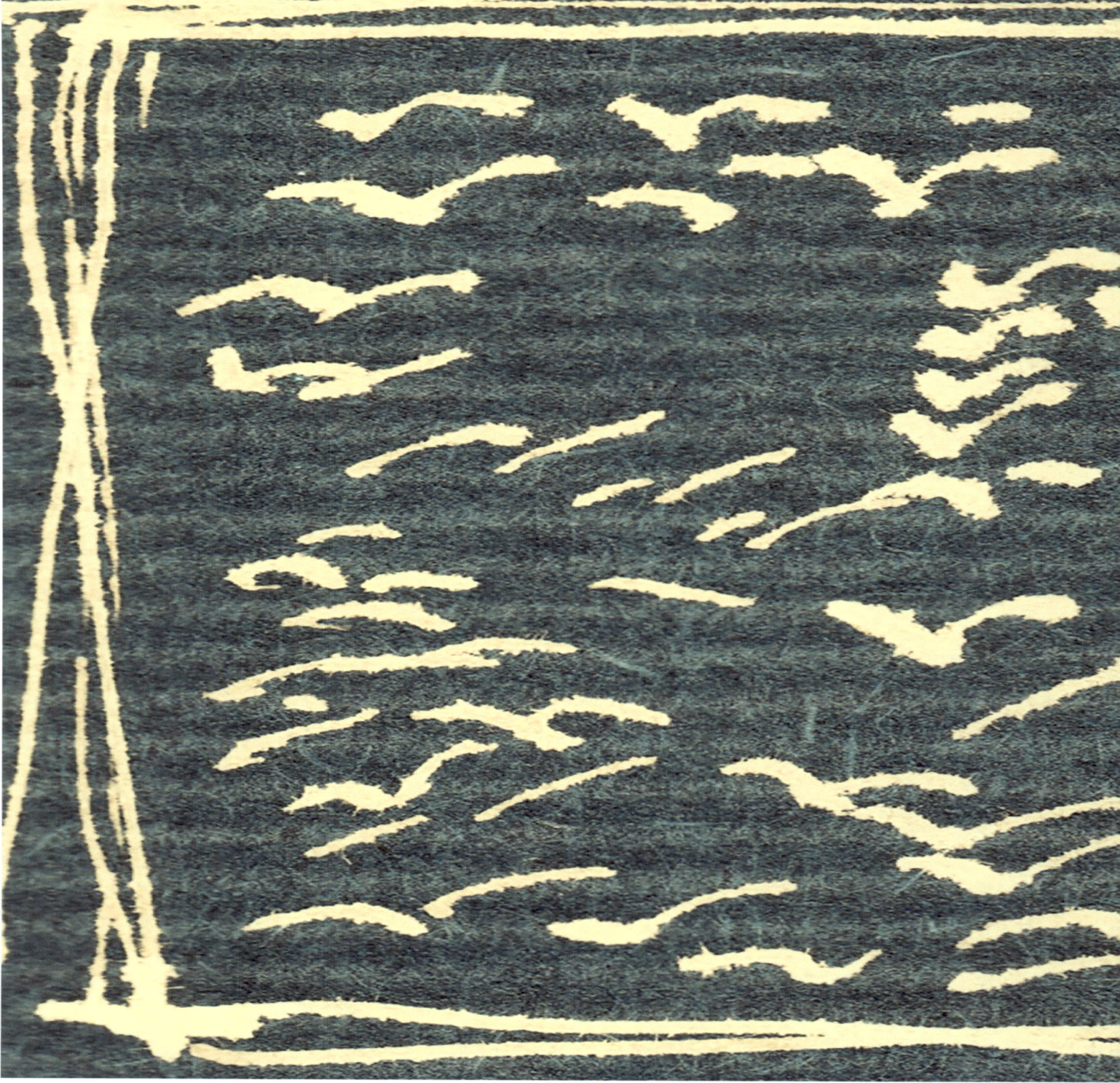

Kam parë një ëndërr sikur
udhëtoja në një dimension të
pa njohur ose të pa ditur nga ato
që dinë. Sikur notoja në vend
pa vend dhe pa qiell,

ëdo gjë ishtë pa materie dhe pa
trup fizik, ëdo gjë ishte grimca
dritash, pa fundit.

I've seen a dream

As I was travelling in a dimension strangely made of

One of those unfamiliar of what I've known

It was like swimming into a place without land, nor a sky too

Everything was matter less and without physical appearance

There were particles of endless lights, as I remember, at least.

1.

nё brёndёsinё e hirtё mёngjesore
shtrihen fushat e kodrat; tё mbuluara
magjishёm nga pёlhura e mjegullёs,
ato pёrmbahen kundrejt shpёrthimit
tё ditёs mёngjesore.
Kёto duken sikur kёrkuesdёm pёr mbulimin dhe
fshehtёsinё e mjegullёs, tё etur janё.
Kёshtu dhe, sytё e mendja ime, shkojnё e humbasin
nё fshehtёsinё e tyre magjepse.

A silent fight seems to begin as the golden light
increases its size an strength
The mountains, agitated by the hidden hunger
of the fog, and encouraged by the golden light,
patiently wait in.
All together, they form a vigorous landscape,
a life of comprehensions
Thus, my eyes slowly lose their view, from the outer
they turn inward into
the landscape of the psyche.
I'm magically fallen in dreams again...
The inner eye demands new occultation.

Into the greyish light of the age

Kindly vanished by the white

Mountains and hills appear different

Although they're still confirmed

All covered by the fog

Painted with a dirty white of

Embracement of the morning

auroral

haze

today

marks

drapery

colour

Light

Gjatë rishkrimit të materialeve që kam
mbledhur, arrij në këtë çast të deshifroj një
nga ëndrrat e mia. [duke u lidhur me arkit-
Ajo ëndërr e cila nuk kishte as tokë as
qiell por një dimension të panditshëm me të
cilin unë mё dukej sikur po notoja në
fluturim tejpërtej përmbledhëse së këtij dim-
nsioni: një vizatim spontan.

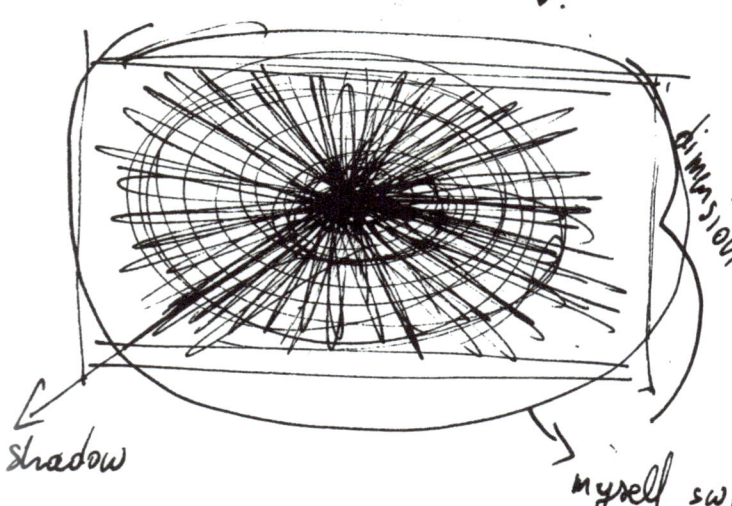

dimension

Shadow

myself swimming
within

an visual representation of
a dream.

Sipas Jung, errësira (hijet) tregon pjesën e
pa njohur (e pazbuluar) të vetveteс së njëriut
pra në rastin tim, pjesën e pa njohur të me
Në fjalë të tjera, tregon se ndërhimi
tashmë ka nisur, dhe se drejtimi ka marrё
ndёrё e duhur.

17 2 '17

Enclosed in the self means no
sound can cross through, neither
smell can touch the sense perception, nor light may penetrate
into the mind, and this is the moment when I search myself within,
uninterrupted to recall the one
I'm asking for. That dream, of no
land and sky but only of strange
appearance, a different world is
its consistency, an abstraction,
and circular movement like a tun-
nel without walls, everything is
unknown to me.

According to C. G Jung said,
is the shadow the archetype that
tells about the unknown, undiscovered part of the self, and this
seems to be the main role of the
dreams, which always try to touch
and awake man's awareness through
consecutive signals that appear
mostly with an opposite content
of what needs to be seen, actual-
ly. This emphasis can be seen in
the out world, in nature and its
mode of making things moving and
changing.

Then, you see these both, the
inner and the outer very similar or better to say made of a
single phenomenon which still is
mystic for us. Same as life under
the water. Thinking about what is
thematised outside, makes me go
into the dream above again, and
then I understand that the dream
tells about the undiscovered part
of myself which runs continuously
like the water into a single dimension, without limits.

*I can clearly tell
that the jour-
ney within myself
has already taken
a further step to
search and learn
about this undis-
covered part of the
self, therefore,
it has become more
than desire though.*

dali: Një nga gjërat që shfaqet shpesh këto ditë
e fundit. Pa e kërkuar ai shfaqet me mua vetë
duke jetuar në territoret e tij.

Shikoj veten duke jetuar në fshatin e tij, në mes të
pjesëve ku sado mëngjes kërkoj për sdo gjë që mund
të jetë e nevojshme, përkrah lumenjve dhe përreth
shtëpisë, duke e punuar në studion time, e kështu me
radhë.

Cila është arsyeja dhe mesazhi i këtij vizioni që kam
këto ditë? Çfarë akoma do të buroj nga kjo thellësi e
brendshme?

Që kur kam fillluar këtë kërkim, shumë gjëra shfaqen
nga brendësia ime (e imit). Janë bërë më i ndjershëm
se çfarë ndodhet përreth meje. Përthithës pa aq se
dhe përcjellës i pastër nga dita në ditë.

Është një dëshirë apo dëshirë e nevojshme?

Një lidhye e fortë dhe e vazhdueshme ka nisur
midis meje dhe brendësi sime, midis synit të, kështu
dhe etij të brendshëm; midis së pjohures dhe së pnjohures
të gjithësisë sime dhe universit komplet.

Zgnoja madhështore

22 02 17.

Another dream is that of the mountain. It appears often these days, and I see myself there, living in its territories, surrounded by nature.

It does not appear only in my dreams, but also in the thoughtful concentration which often I do myself the moment I'm awake. Again, I see myself moving on its great shape, among the woods, searching about something, in need of something, rivers, and I see houses less popular. Walking, walking to find, observing to understand.

-What is the reason?
-What is the coming content?

I started searching myself, therefore many things appear different than before, and sometimes their ''mutation'' developed is seen. The more determined and consecutive, I'm in pursuing, the more understandable they become. I feel as I'm becoming rather sensitive to all around me or my conscious has changed its language, and I experience all differently since.

-Is this a desire or a spiritual necessity?

A strong connection, I feel; a self-reflective passage, from the one to the whole, and going back again…

Water connected to waters, continuously transformed, eternally returning back; roots of a spiritual, unintelligible, and invisible privilege, a particle of constellation, man's soul which grows in the One an the Whole.

"The iliaster is without doubt a spiritual, invisible principle although it is also something like prima materia, which, however, in alchemical usage by no means corresponds to what we understand by matter. For the alchemist the prima materia was the 'homidium radicale' (radical moisture), the water, it was also called the 'soul' of the substance, the sperma mundi, Adam's tree of paradise with its many flowers, which grows on the sea, the round body from the centre, Adam and the accursed man, the hermaphrodic monster, the One and the root of itself, the All, and so on".

Edwin 22nd

Adobe scrt.

Gopro camera.   → 4 dk. quality film.

Linda → software tools.

as a group-essence

d moder man.

derson.

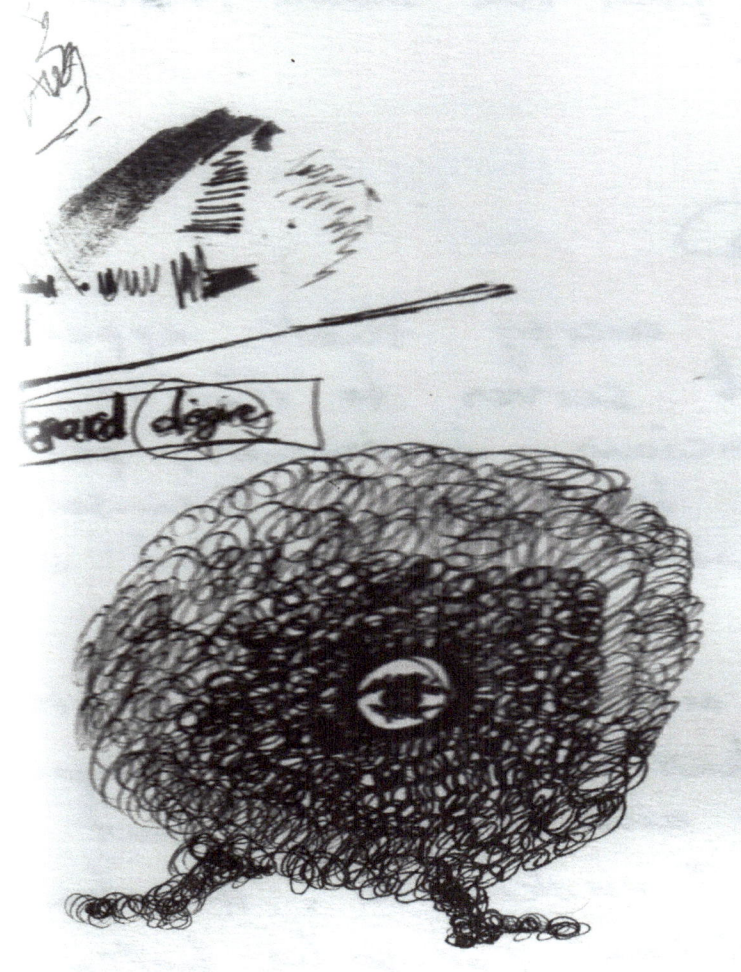

"Transparent glass is something like solidified water or air, both of which are synonyms for the spirit. The alchemical retort is, therefore, equivalent to the 'anima mundi', which according to an old alchemical conception surrounds the cosmos".

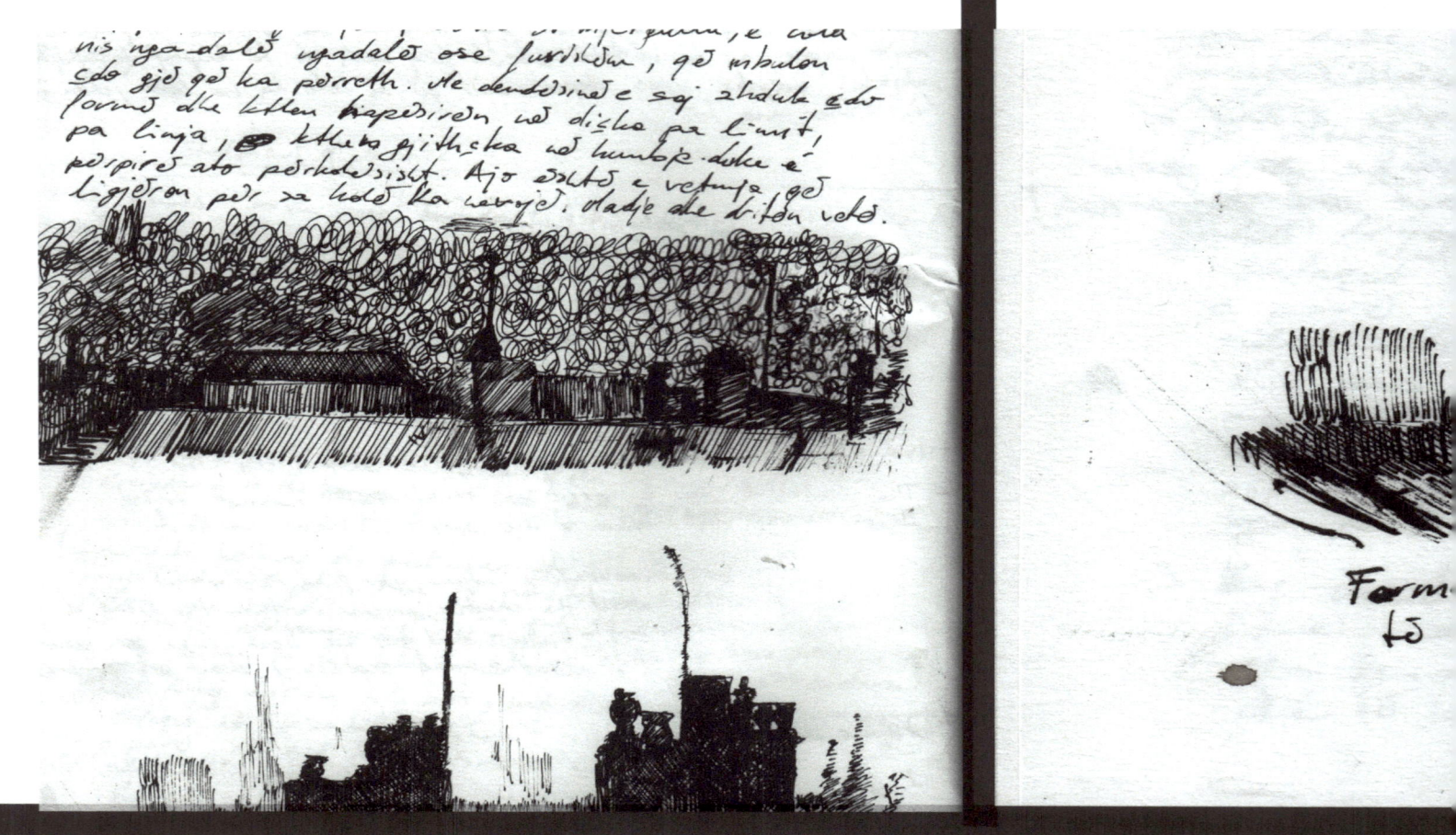

A sensation starts slowly focusing to the outer, while the nebulous matter comes from the sea towards the city. It feels like a magic substance that conquers the havens, and I perceive it as the breath of another liquid form; WATER! There is short period of governance given to it, even the light knees before its majesty. Although it
retires after a while, it will come back again with by a silent temperament. The most solid and strongest forms will always be distinct among others; despite the dense fog which is extended throughout the entire city, their shapes may stand there, frozen in time as concrete blocks, and as well as may turn suddenly into dust.

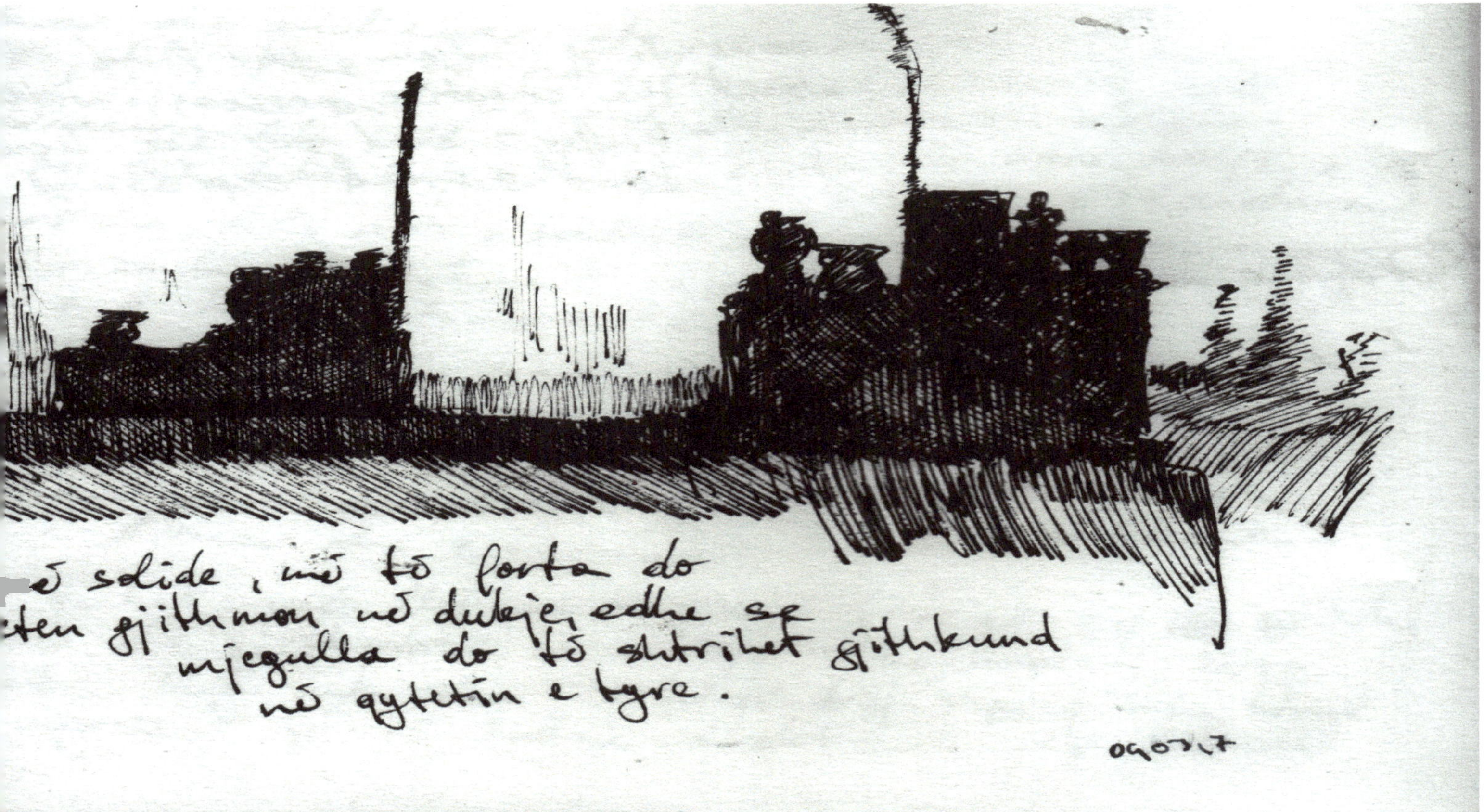

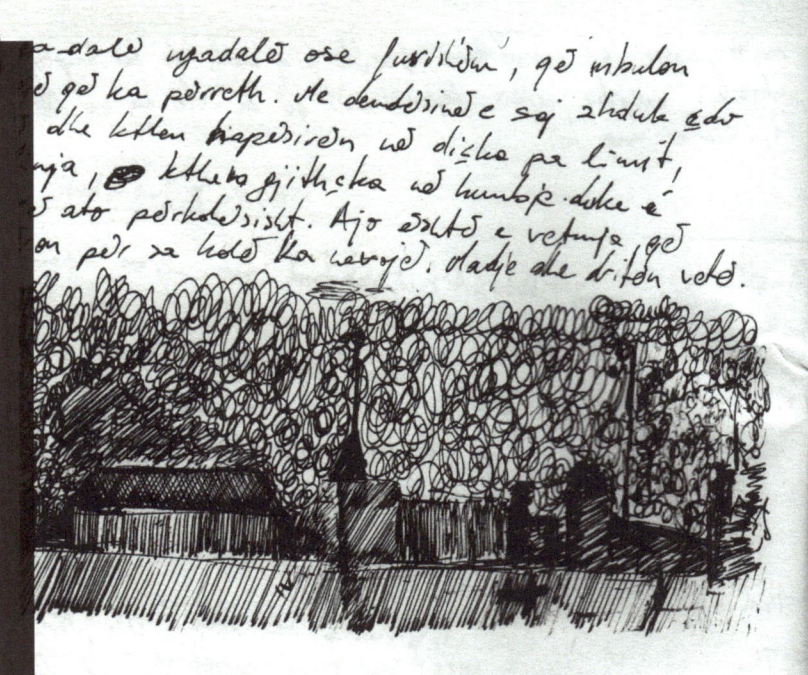

ō solide, më tō forta do
ten gjithmon në dukje, edhe se
mjegulla do tō shtrihet gjithkund
në qytetin e tyre.

ogosit

a-dalō ngadalō ose furtliōn, gō mbulon
ō gō ka pērreth. Me dendōsinō e saj zhduke edv
dke kthen hapōsirōn nō dicka pa limit,
ja, @ kthen gjithcka nō hunōp. duke ē
s ato pōrkōbēsisht. Ajo ōxtō e vetmja gō
on pōr sa holō ka nervjō. dadje dke dritōn veld.

[influential memories have
the same structure and func-
tion, and can affect one's
behavior patterns until
the end of his life, unless
whether an analysis begins
they lose the strength, and
the content found can then
be beneficial]

i. Eshtë e vështirë, mos thena që shumë
dhimbse, të gjithmonë brenda vedes. Gruadhini.
Eshtë gjithmonë e më pranë sa herë që
zhgjen dhellë e më shellë.

Ktuy gjej plot bukuri nga here, por dhe egz
bukuri mos kthen nd ujd mëlankali dhe
dhimbje; po ankta gjej dashuri td veshuu
he ujd dhimbje td thnensoshme, e më
mos lotoj.

31 / 0

It is hard to find, therefore less popular. While you're digging inside yourself there is an insanity portion of the psyche that accompanies you closely throughout the path you're driven to a deeper and deeper self-reflection.

Beauty can be found in there too, a slight sign of hope, but even this turns itself to melancholy. Love becomes pain too, then after I cry...

ALL these movements that one does in himself are employed by the mechanism of his psyche which unlocks the force of energy, a helpful means for a stronger consciousness.
   The soul is a migrant, a born and restless traveller which seeks for any kind of experience that fulfil is desires, and cannot be stopped doing so, but only directed. That is something I cannot explain, yet.

But ku levirzja 1 2 3 4 5 6 7 8 9 0

2. Any movement can unlock

Ener

the hau

physic

ku levirzja 1 2 3 4 5 6 7 8 9 0

ku levirzja ndah i-1

$1 = 1$
$0 = 0$ ndah midis.

$0 = 1$ ku levirzja

$b = b$

But the main 'mee

~~its thinking~~ is

is

is is

is is

is is
something
that becomes
nothing !?

070317

Energy unlocked the hands and ultimately a form kind

Any movement can unlock ...the energy that goes

the every then transmitted through

the hands and ultimately a form kind

hands
body
body and moving
physic
body

is is
that becomes
nothing !?

unlocked

...the energy that /

the energy / then / goes transmitted through

and / ultimately, a form kind

of visible / a form is given there

here   through tools.
                              hands
                              body

...anism is the body and nothing.
                         physic
a mechanism   body
a trasmiter   & 11 16
li thing .
something
that becomes
nothing .

07 0317

energy unlocked

2. Any ...... can unlock ...the energy that
goes
... the energy then transmitted through
a form kind
... form is given there
through tools.
hands
body
physic
body
the body and ...
physic
body
& 11 16
body

1. Fillova të marr një rrugë
rrugë që tejkalon të shikuarit
brenda në thellësitë e unit tim.

2.

fillim	kudo	vend	pavdud
rrugë	dritë	vetëm	energji
errësirë	lidhje	gjithka	ndërgjegje ngorac
drejtim	përjetim	2bulim	materie mendim
		kërkim	trup emocion shijim
			dhimbje mëndje
idea	figura		psikologji, dashuri musik
dija			e panjohur figurë
e panjohura			rilindje, filozofi
e njohura	unë, ata, ne		plot bosh
2gjini			përplasje
			getësi
kapërcim, krijim, frymëzim			kundërshtim.

3.

energjia

figura → fillim → rrugë → errësirë → kudo
→ dritë → 2bulim
lidhje → idea
emocion → krijim → kërkim → ndërgjegje + → plot
dashuri × → dhimbje × → pavdud ×
psikologji → mëndje → filozofi → përplasje
unë ne ata ti / K n a t / unë ti ne ata / U t K a
e panjohura → 2gjidhje → dije → kapërcim
frymëzim
bosh → vend → i panjohur

I've started a way that exceeds the ordinary idea about self-viewing by which I can consciously touch forbidden memories, and extract from them the most precious material, key points that open the doors of inner energy.

start, everywhere, way, dark, light, direction, connection, experiencing, land, alone, everything, discovering, exploring, nowhere, energy, matter, body, lack, struggling, emotion, wound, psyche, releasing, mind, love, music, idea, reborn, unknown, myself, image, void, inspiration, we, creation, peace, knowledge, against, complite.

The artist must deal with a con
heights means simultaneously to

There is not only what is shown at first in things, the eye must
change the seeing-angle continuously and the weight of ages should
be taken in consideration, any relation with the circularity of life.

ᴹ

centric universe where to seek the

explore the depths.   p 31

The artist must go underneath and deeper into the core of things in order to bring in the surface the hidden components, to reveal parts of the life which are valuable elements for sake of human evolution.

-What does it mean?

This is a question that follows often with me, which means that there is a necessity to understand firstly, before accepting things after. Feeling is what tells you whether something is agreeable or not. Is how my feelings start speaking about artworks made by computers, something that for the moment I don't really feel as something that I want deal with. I am not attracted by this manner of making because it hasn't anything in which I release energy through my hands, I can not touch it, there is no conversation between us, and there is no magic for me to deal with.

    Thus, you understand the smell of the colours, the noisy pencil, the touch of the canvas, the struggling with dilemma, finding ways to create the most difficult forms, all about the process and others; everything you are/have as a human being, and whilst you try to give a shape or colours, it gives you back meaningful lectures. A static way of working it is not for me, I've realized, I want to feel every step, to fight with the canvas, to eat the charcoal, to express haw wonderful the light is, to live within colours, I want to see them growing and listen to their stories, because is where I find freedom without interruptions

1. Open the space for the public.? -- • Reflection + people bringing together

Andry ken

Çfarë ndodësi ka gjithë ky lloj arti për mua?

Nuk ndiej aspak tërhegje dhe magjepsje nga kjo stil arti. Çka që nuk përthith, trypin dhe lvizjet e etij duke krijuar, loje dhe bërje me anë të duarve, kuntakti me sytë dhe energjitë, e cila është e lëshuar në materian e punës; ndse nuk ndiej dhe përjetoj gjithë këtë përgjat kohës që punoj (krij.), ka asnjë rëndësi të bie dalur për të ndryshuar stilin, për mua nuk dhe llojin e artit që bëj.

Si dr që të jetë, të dijë se shohah në botet dhe me artin sot (dijehidel) nuk është, për keq si ndhuri, përkundrazi.

bols.

To go deep in self-meditation about the direction that I want to take in my artistic creativity, it means to keep records of my productivity and to understand better my character. I assume that's very important for a personal development as an artist, and also pursuing the same process in myself .will benefit the evolution of my being a human.

Despite the personal preferences, to know about what's happening in the art world, is not futile, in contrary, it is useful knowledge that helps me to understand my own work, as well as its strength and weakness, as well as the importance of the diversity found in the world.

An artist may take may directions, but there is only in one thing that he must obey and work for, and that is the Truth.

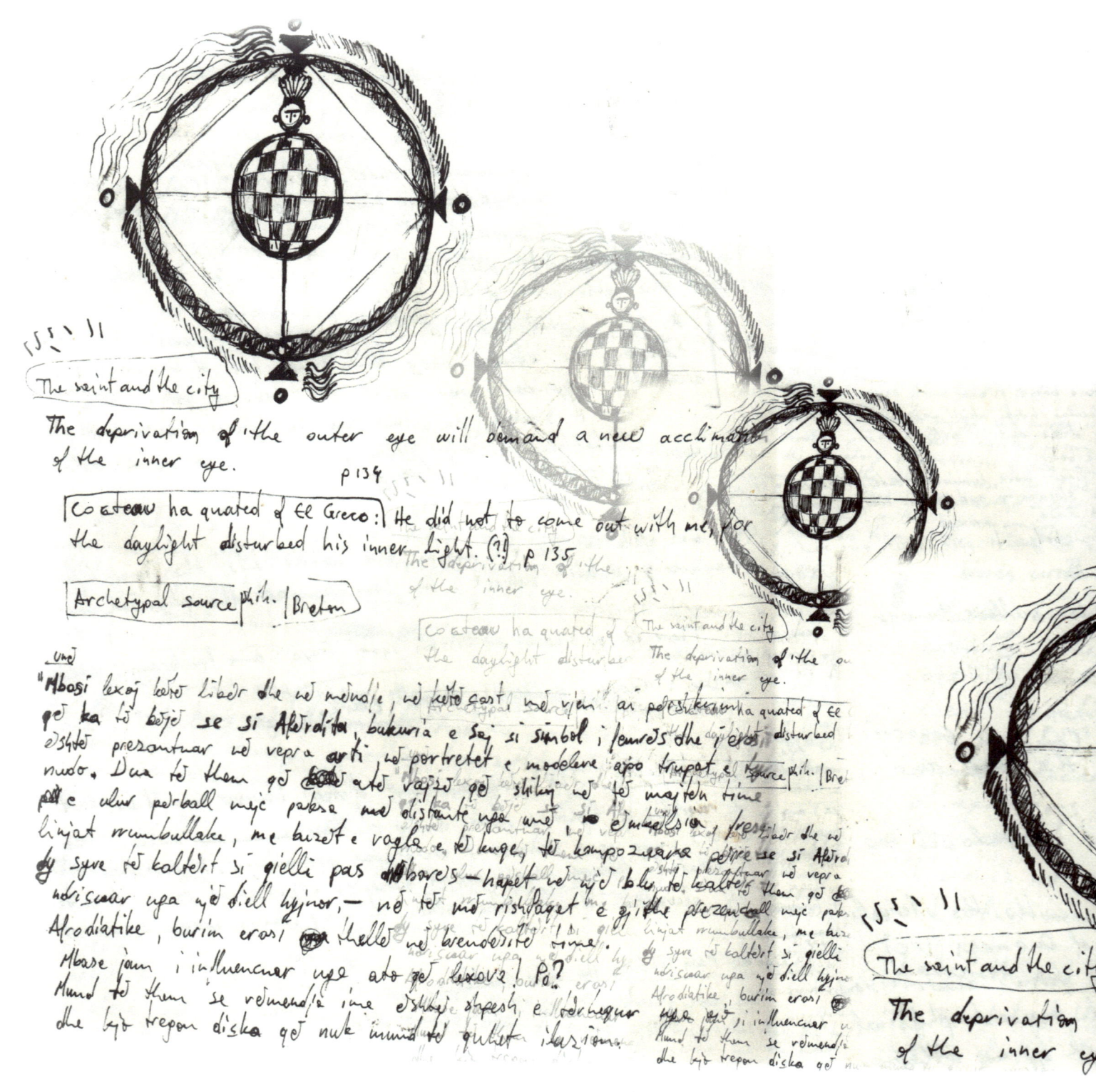

The saint and the city

The saint and the city

The deprivation of the outer eye will demand a new acclima[tion] of the inner eye.

p 134

Cocteau ha quoted of El Greco: He did not to come out with me, for the daylight disturbed his inner light. (?) p 135

Archetypal source phil. | Breton

"Mbasi lexoj këtë libër dhe më mundoje, në këtë rast më vjen ai përshtëkrimi që ka të bëjë se si Afërdita, bukuria e saj si simbol i femrës dhe që është prezantuar në vepra arti në portretet e modeleve apo trupat nudo. Dua të them që ato vajza që stilizën në të majtën time e ulur përball mejc paksa me distantë upa une — emocion linjat rrumbullake, me buzët e vogla e të kuqe, të kompozuara dy syve të kaltërt si qielli pas dëborës — hapet në një blu ndiscuar upa një diell hyjnor, — në të më rishfaqet e gjithe prezentall mejc pak Afrodiatike, burim erosi më thellë në brendësitë time.

Mbase jam i influencuar upa ato që lexova! Po? Mund të them se rëmendja ime është shpesh e ndërhequr dhe lyt tregon diska që nuk inmindatë qullet ilazionu."

After reading this chapter, in my mind comes the description of Aphrodite the Greek goddess of love, beauty, pleasure, and pro-creation. She has become the motive of many artists' work, and it is also the motive that I've very used in my works too. One can see that there is a goddess beyond every woman's eye.

And then I would say that when inner eye can cross beyond the surface and can possibly discover a totally different world from that of the outer, it can add another lens to the out-er eye which makes possible to observe the hidden dimension of one's psyche, although it demands continual exercise and dif-ferent state of mind of that so called normal. How this inner eyes sees, have a look at Art of 19th century, and clearly seen in Goya's works as well.

Consequently, one becomes more sensi-tive towards the nu-minous aspects of the same thing, and it is required if one wants to discover the hid-den roots where real sense of living feeds every idea which give life to our solely spirit.

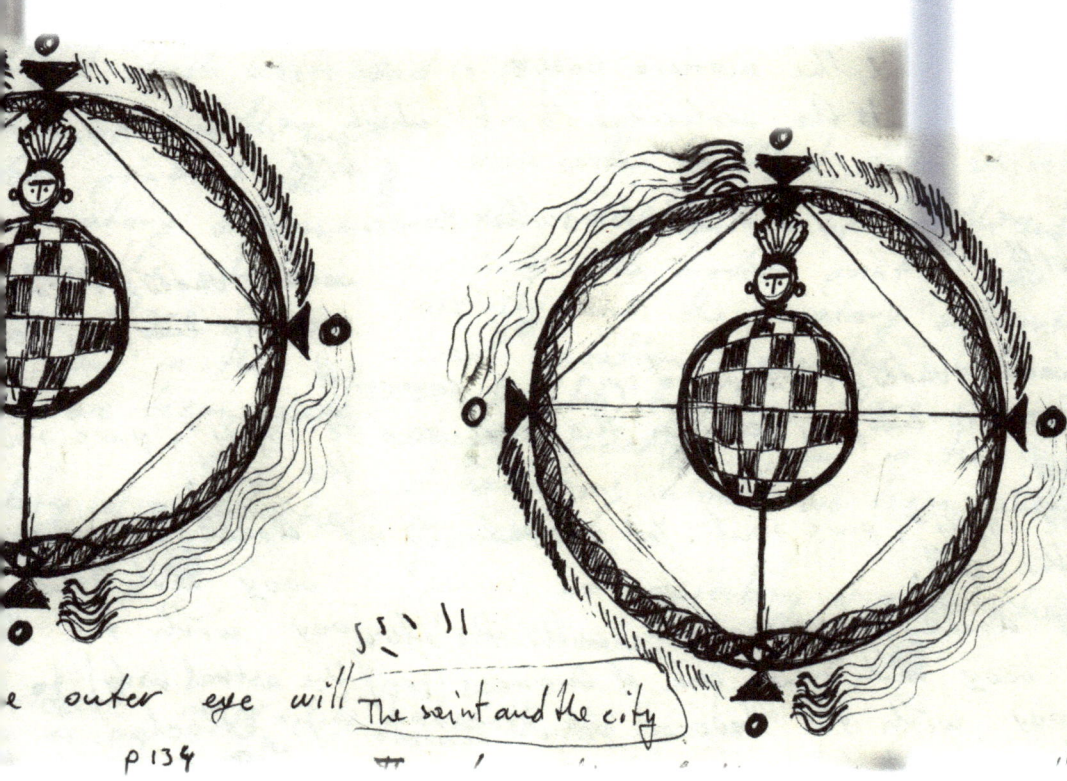

e outer eye will The saint and the city

p 134

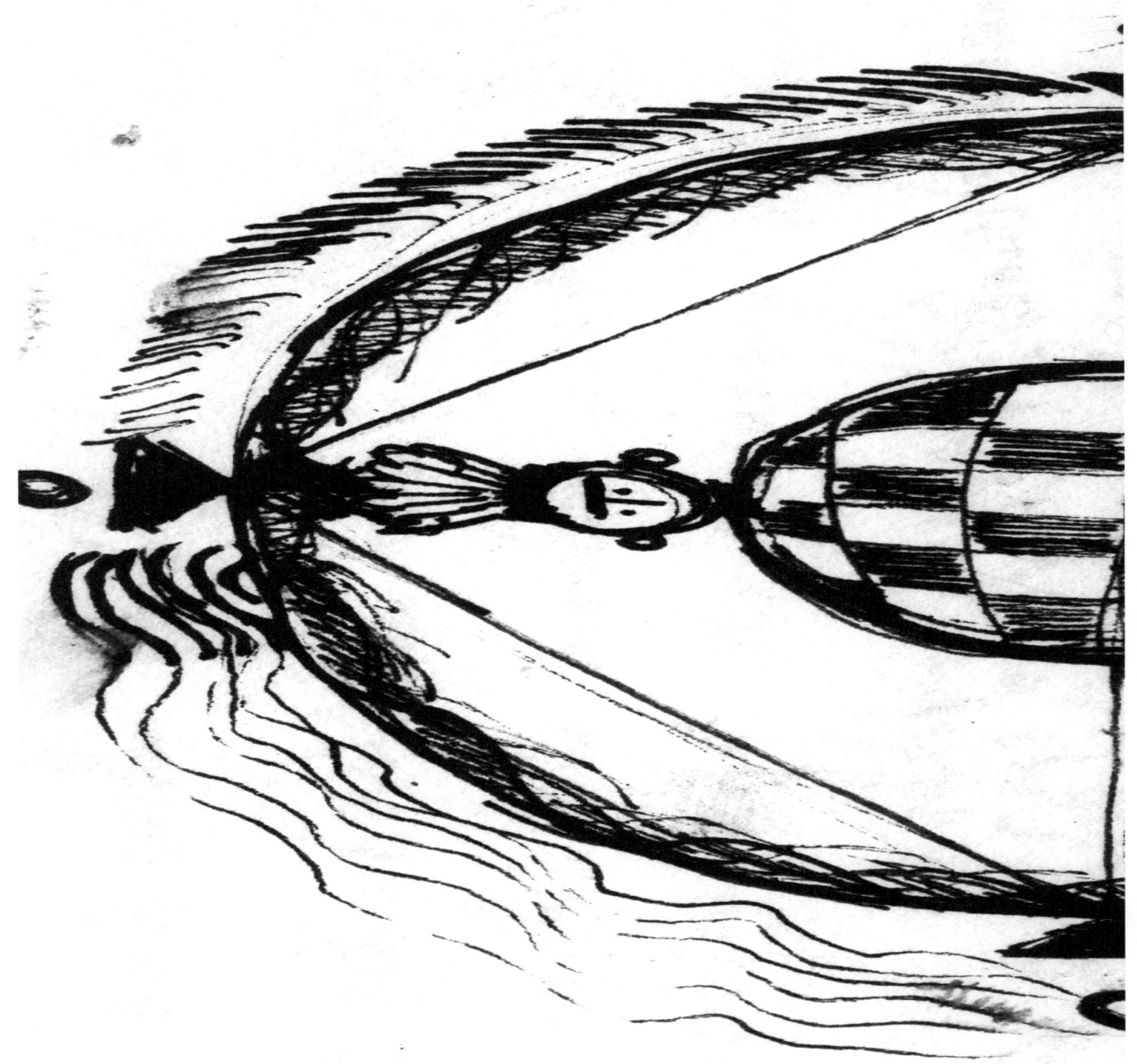

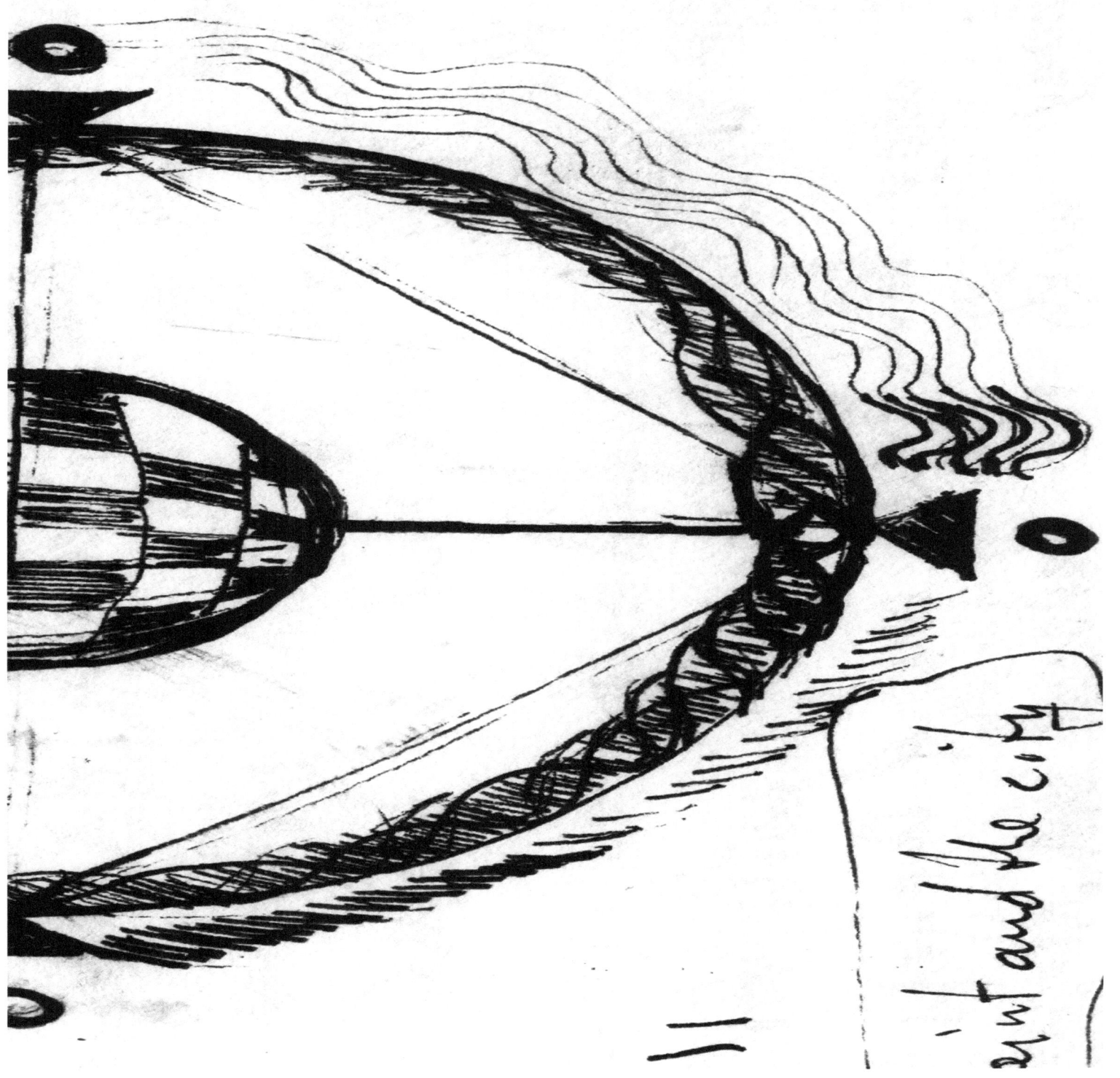

The inner eye.
a depicting interpretation
of "The rose window
of the cathedral of
Notre Dame, Paris"
found in the book
P. ?

= simbolet e Sylaquren gjitd rruges.
1. Kotumba
2. falaja
3. Piramida.
4. Portreti iV.

The tree
of symbols as same as the philosophical tree
(tree of Life)

Thus, our dreams life creates a meandering
pattern in which individual strands or tendencies
become visible, then vanish, then return again.

P.161.

The self can be defined as an inner guiding factor
that is different from the conscious personality,
and that can be grasped only through the investigation
one's dreams. (...) How far it develops depends
wether or not the ego is willing to listen to the messages
of the self. (...) Great man becomes more real within the
receptive person than in those who neglect him.
Such a person also becomes a more complet human being.

p. 162

Whether this part of the self can be defined as spiritual guiding factor, it consists too, of an unconscious uncontrolled part as a significant factor that can lead to a better a fulfilled investigation of one's dreams and spontaneous desires that appear. Even the ego is alive before it is aware of its being, it can be directed and turned into a key that helps in opening the doors of unconscious of the self, where great information is held in, waiting to be unfold.

A person becomes a more complete human being, not only by investigation of his dreams, but also being aware that he himself is found within other human being, even partly.

When one understands that all these pieces of the self are as similar as of those of the nature, that he himself is found in every single action of other people, and that all these together are interlinked between them, and that no one can be without the other, consequently I believe of 'Ouroboros', as incarnation of all these happenings into one single creature.

"Imagine the Earth turning around itself, and the Sun, at the same time"

kutia - piramidet.

0.

drita → zjarri

— hyrja
sqit

bashkë... ajri

balta.

baza e piramides

ajri   uji

bashkimi
→

balta   zjarri

- hyrje është e zënë nga një
kristal (.... përkadiesi i nj. f)
i cili nuk ndalon dritën
(zjarri energji) përkundrasi e
filtron atë dhe e kthen
në fungi shndërruese, kalon
hyn në bashkëveprim me
ajrin i cili me anë të djegjes
shndërrohet në frymë
me anë të sëciles balta merr
formë dhe mund gravitetim.

Due to this circularity is how the idea takes form, and belongs within our daily life.

The idea; represents the fluidity of thoughts which must be kept busy, otherwise it would been futile to wear this limited body; it is made of dreams and desires, of everything known and unknown, and according to our force of belief it may turn into a shell of steel (prison) or it may become a transparent limitless house for the soul (where one can go in and out freely).

One does not just decrease by analysing it but can finds an endless world of spiritual light and himself dissolved in many parts made of the same nature, where an element can possibly spring out towards renovation of the self, later.
[energy travels in time by four elements, dissolving and solidifying them again and again]

Air

Water

Fire

Soil

The idea is what makes a man feeling and understanding the real sense of things in life R. W Emerson.

The idea consists

Thoughts

Present

and future

Experiences

And

influences

The past time of all

warmth

Memory and awaren

THE TREE OF LIFE THE TREE OF PHYSIS

Environment

Happenings

surroundings ...

idea.

mendimi
të menduarit.

+ ardhmëria.

perjetimin + gjendjet

e kaluara
+ ngacmimet

kujtesa.

+ dije

ambienti

dhe historia + ndodhitë
influencat që rrethojnë

THE PHILOSOPHICAL TREE THE PSYCHOLOGICAL TREE TREE OF EVERYTHING

A BRIDGE BY CURRENT OF CONNECTION

dbas çdo sipërfaqe ka diçka më
më shumë se thjeshtë ajo që dukojnë
me të parën herë.
● Çdo, qoftë materiale ose jo
mbar një botë të tërë përtej
pamjes. Zbërthimi dhe kuptimi i
saj sjell dije më vete dhe botën
emësirën e pavetëdijes edhe më të
ndritshme. Kjo është e duhur
zhdërrimi se vetëdijia vrientohet nga pavetëdija.

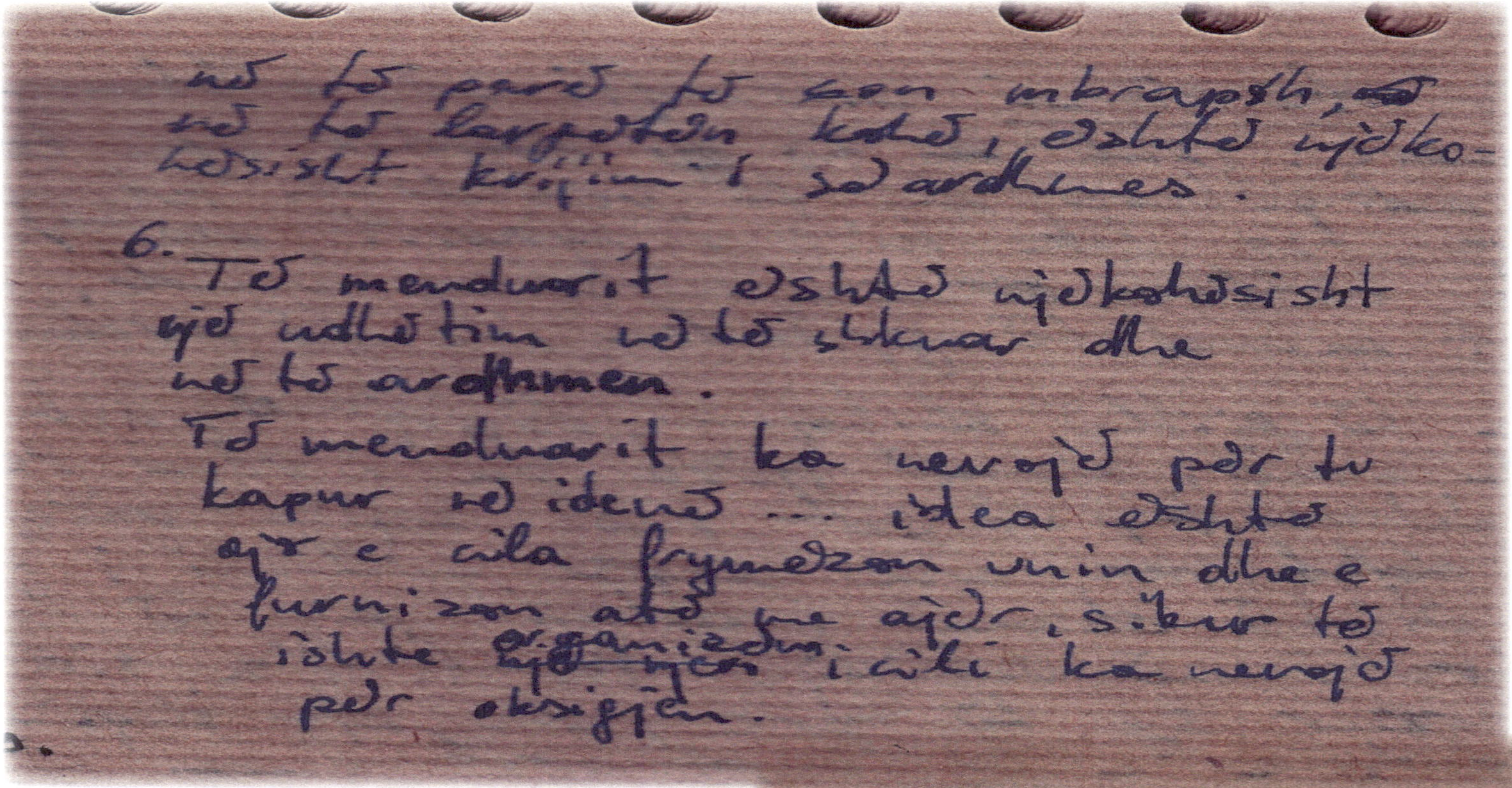

në të parë të saj mbrapsht, në këtë largësi kohë, është njëko-hësisht kujtim i së ardhmes.

6. Të menduarit është njëkohësisht një udhëtim në të shkuar dhe në të ardhmen.
Të menduarit ka nevojë për të kapur një idenë ... idea është një e cila frymëzon unin dhe e furnizon atë me ajër, si ku të ishte organizëm i cili ka nevojë për oksigjen.

Under the soil, there has much to discover; erecting the skin of the common mid-desert can be discovered a great world of meaningful information. The dark unconscious can be enlightened by digging and understanding of its world, and this is the channel that consciousness follows to a better view of the unknown content of the self within.

Like an iceberg (Freud;-mind as an iceberg), the most important part of the mind is the part that you cannot see. It takes you to the very past time, backwards, while without noticing you go forwards building a path of past and present which is future, simultaneously.

We have seen from a number of sources that the numinous, the spiritual, the unknown or the unintelligible can often have an uneasy relationship with interpretative systems operating within a largely secular, rationalist culture. We must look for the depth in the unintelligible. (Kuspit)

Is the thinking that takes a journey through all levels of psyche, and every significant element needs to be captured within an ideal thought, for it is what feed the self of inspiration for exploring the unknown that is accompanied by the personal interpretative system.

What happens to us when art connects to the unconscious

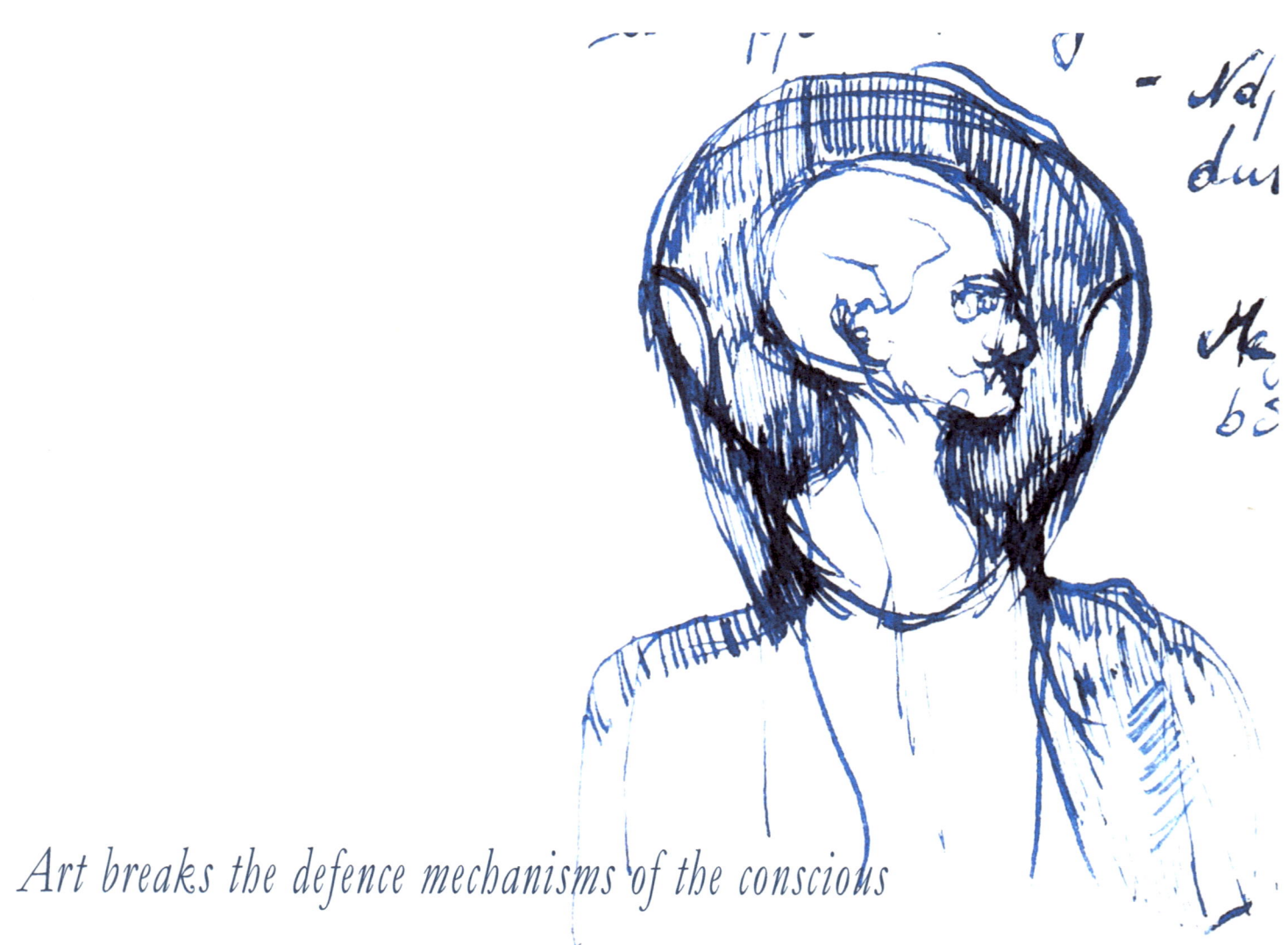

Art breaks the defence mechanisms of the conscious

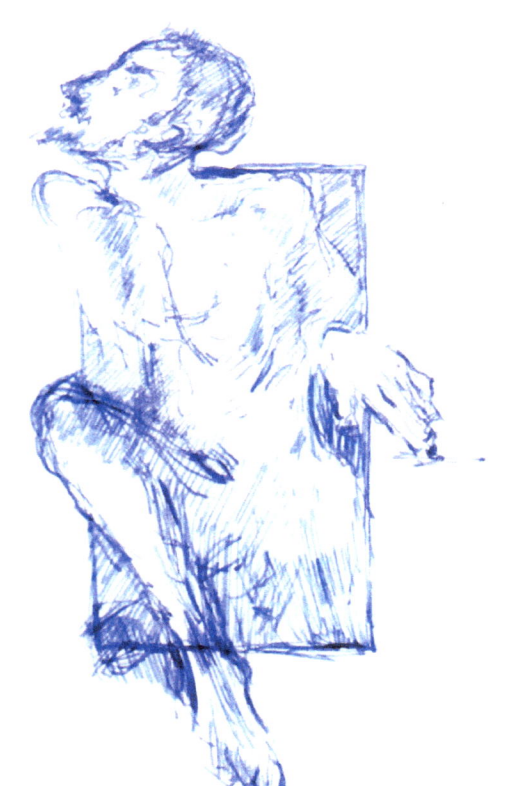

Say.

I feel as I want to leave
to go away
from this window
to breake
to destroy
each border that I'm contained within

The works of R. W. Emerson.
- Letters and Social aims.
· Greatness.

"There is a price which we are all
aiming at, and the more power and good-
ness we have, so much more energy of that
aim. Every human being has a right to it,
and in the pursuit we do not stand in each
other's way. For it has a long scale of
degrees, a wide variety of views, and every
aspirant, by his success in the pursuit,
does not hider but helps his compettitors.
I might call it Completness, but that is
later, — perhaps adjourned for ages.
It is the fulfilment of a natural
tedency in each man. It is a fruit-
ful study.   p. 266

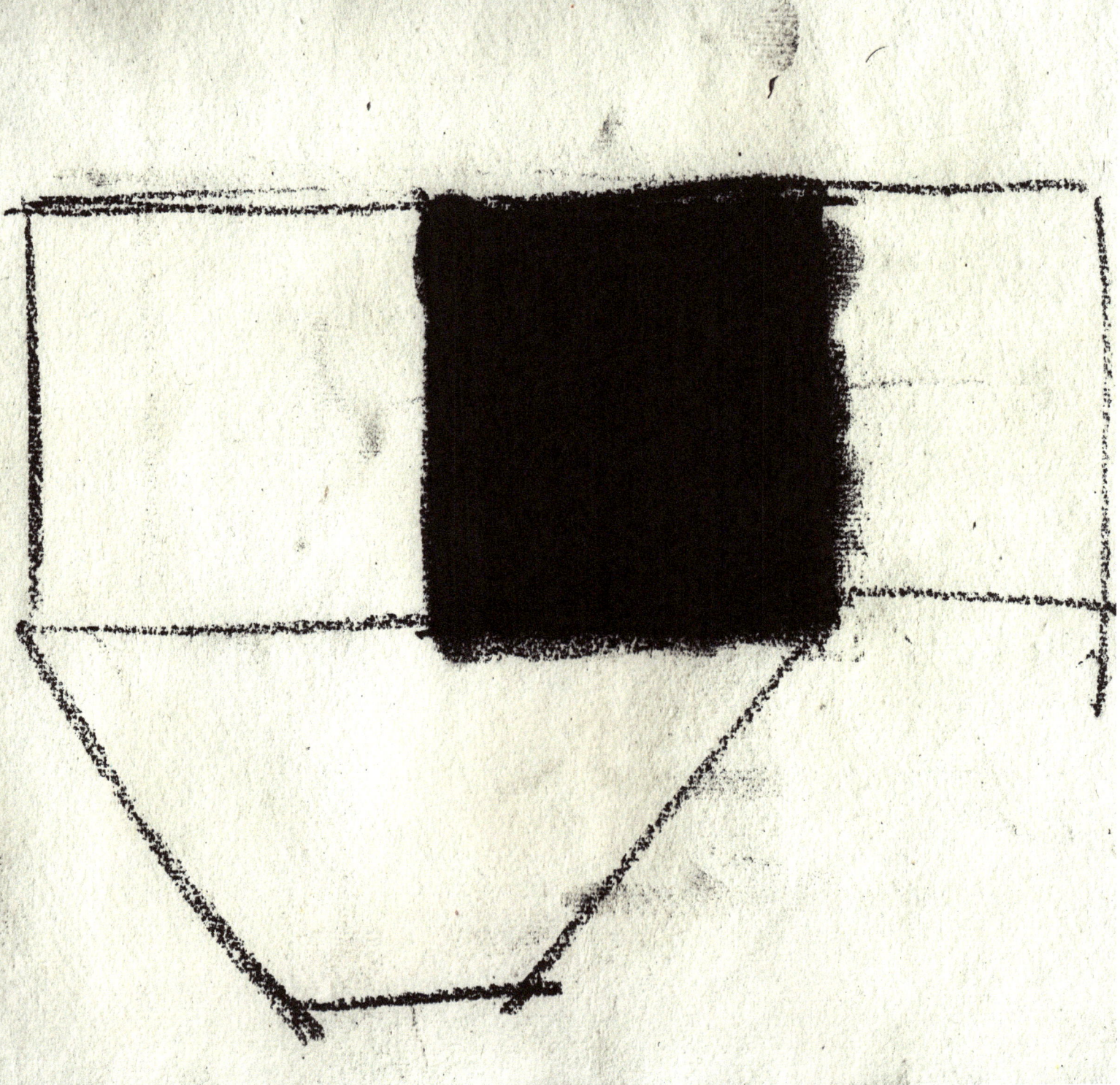

sources

Alan Watts. https://www.youtube.com/watch?v=NWnVpUpehRI&t=19s&list=PLPtY6tnHCLOigAiz7-PnVEDlT9WZO3OiY&index=2

Bachelard, G. and Frye, N. (n.d.). The psychoanalysis of fire. 1st ed. [ebook] pp.1-13. Available at: http://unit2theory.pbworks.com/f/BachelardPsycho.%20of%20 Fire.pdf [Accessed 11 Mar. 2017].

Bergson, H. (1975). Mind-energy: lectures & essays .... 1st ed. [Place of publication not identified]: [publisher not identified], pp.55-195.

Emerson, R. (1912). Society and solitude. 1st ed. Boston: Jefferson.

En.wikipedia.org. (2017). Earth's rotation. [online] Available at: https://en.wikipedia.org/wiki/Earth%27s_rotation [Accessed 22 Apr. 2017].

Evans, M. (2015). An aesthetic of the unknown. International Journal of Jungian Studies, [online] 7(1), pp.19-32. Available at: http://www.tandfonline.com/loi/ rijj20 [Accessed 21Feb. 2017].

Gauguin, P. and Guérin, D. (1996). The writings of a savage 1st ed. New York: Da Capo Press.

Harris, W. (2017). HERACLITUS. The Complete Fragments. 1st ed. [ebook] Middlebury: Middlebury College, pp.1-58. Available at: http://community.middle-bury.edu/~harris/Philosophy/heraclitus.pdf [Accessed 5 Mar. 2017].

Jung, C. and Franz, M. (1976). Man and his symbols. 13th ed. New York: Dell Publishing, p.38.

Jung, C., Read, H., Fordham, M. and Adler, G. (1967). The collected works of C.G. Jung. 13th ed. Princeton, N.J.: Princeton University Press, pp.194-253.

Klee, P. and Spiller, J. (1969). The thinking eye. 1st ed. London: Lund Humphries, pp.1-40.

Martin Antonetti - Artists Books: A Definition for the 21st Century https://www.youtube.com/watch?v=sYEDJpYr1e4&t=2046s&list=PLPtY6tnHCLOigAiz-7PnVEDlT9WZO3OiY&index=10

McLeod, S. (2009). Unconscious Mind | Simply Psychology. [online] Simplypsychology.org. Available at: https://www.simplypsychology.org/unconscious-mind.html [Accessed 3 Feb. 2017].

Rosenblum, R., Stevens, M. and Dumas, A. (2000). 1900. 1st ed. New York: H.N.

Schwartz, P. (1977). Art and the occult. 1st ed. London: Unwin Paperbacks, pp.1-6.

The Book's Undoing: Dieter Roth's Artist's Books
https://www.youtube.com/watch?v=_XVe5hd81IU&list=PLPtY6tnHCLOigAiz7-PnVEDlT9WZO3OiY&index=9

Van den Berk. and Tjeu. (2012). Jung on art : the autonomy of the creative drive. 1st ed. East Sussex: Routledge, p.6.

Winn, S. (2007). What happens to us when art connects to the unconscious. [online] SFGate. Available at: http://www.sfgate.com/entertainment/article/What-hap-pens-to-us-when-art-connects-to-the-2591269.php [Accessed 10 Mar. 2017].

www.ingramcontent.com/pod-product-compliance
Lightning Source LLC
Chambersburg PA
CBHW051027180526
45172CB00002B/495